W9-CHV-985

Asthma

Titles in the Diseases and Disorders series include:

Acne
ADHD
Alcoholism
Allergies
Amnesia
Anorexia and Bulimia
Anxiety Disorders
Asperger's Syndrome
Autism
Blindness
Brain Trauma
Brain Tumors
Cancer
Cerebral Palsy
Cervical Cancer
Childhood Obesity
Dementia
Depression
Diabetes
Epilepsy
Hepatitis
Human Papillomavirus (HPV)

Infectious Mononucleosis
Leukemia
Malnutrition
Mental Retardation
Migraines
MRSA
Multiple Sclerosis
Personality Disorders
Phobias
Plague
Post Traumatic Stress
   Disorder
Prostate Cancer
Sexually Transmitted
   Diseases
Skin Cancer
Speech Disorders
Sports Injuries
Sudden Infant Death
   Syndrome
Thyroid Disorders

DISEASES & DISORDERS

Asthma

Barbara Sheen

LUCENT BOOKS
A part of Gale, Cengage Learning

GALE
CENGAGE Learning

Detroit • New York • San Francisco • New Haven, Conn • Waterville, Maine • London

GALE
CENGAGE Learning™

© 2011 Gale, Cengage Learning

LIBRARY OF CONGRESS CATALOGING-IN-PUBLICATION DATA

Sheen, Barbara.
  Asthma / by Barbara Sheen.
    p. cm. -- (Diseases & Disorders)
  Includes bibliographical references and index.
  ISBN 978-1-4205-0591-7 (hardcover : alk. paper) 1. Asthma--Juvenile literature. I. Title.
  RC591.S534 2011
  616.2'38--dc22

                                                                    2010047340

Lucent Books
27500 Drake Rd
Farmington Hills MI 48331

ISBN-13: 978-1-4205-0591-7
ISBN-10: 1-4205-0591-2

Printed in the United States of America
1 2 3 4 5 6 7 15 14 13 12 11

Printed by Bang Printing, Brainerd, MN, 1ˢᵗ Ptg., 03/2011

Table of Contents

"The Most Difficult Puzzles Ever Devised"

Charles Best, one of the pioneers in the search for a cure for diabetes, once explained what it is about medical research that intrigued him so. "It's not just the gratification of knowing one is helping people," he confided, "although that probably is a more heroic and selfless motivation. Those feelings may enter in, but truly, what I find best is the feeling of going toe to toe with nature, of trying to solve the most difficult puzzles ever devised. The answers are there somewhere, those keys that will solve the puzzle and make the patient well. But how will those keys be found?"

Since the dawn of civilization, nothing has so puzzled people—and often frightened them, as well—as the onset of illness in a body or mind that had seemed healthy before. A seizure, the inability of a heart to pump, the sudden deterioration of muscle tone in a small child—being unable to reverse such conditions or even to understand why they occur was unspeakably frustrating to healers. Even before there were names for such conditions, even before they were understood at all, each was a reminder of how complex the human body was, and how vulnerable.

While our grappling with understanding diseases has been frustrating at times, it has also provided some of humankind's most heroic accomplishments. Alexander Fleming's accidental discovery in 1928 of a mold that could be turned into penicillin has resulted in the saving of untold millions of lives. The isolation of the enzyme insulin has reversed what was once a death sentence for anyone with diabetes. There have also been great strides in combating conditions for which there is not yet a cure. Medicines can help AIDS patients live longer, diagnostic tools such as mammography and ultrasounds can help doctors find tumors while they are treatable, and laser surgery techniques have made the most intricate, minute operations routine.

This "toe-to-toe" competition with diseases and disorders is even more remarkable when seen in a historical continuum. An astonishing amount of progress has been made in a very short time. Just two hundred years ago, the existence of germs as a cause of some diseases was unknown. In fact, it was less than 150 years ago that a British surgeon named Joseph Lister had difficulty persuading his fellow doctors that washing their hands before delivering a baby might increase the chances of a healthy delivery (especially if they had just attended to a diseased patient)!

Each book in Lucent's Diseases and Disorders series explores a disease or disorder and the knowledge that has been accumulated (or discarded) by doctors through the years. Each book also examines the tools used for pinpointing a diagnosis, as well as the various means that are used to treat or cure a disease. Finally, new ideas are presented—techniques or medicines that may be on the horizon.

Frustration and disappointment are still part of medicine, for not every disease or condition can be cured or prevented. But the limitations of knowledge are being pushed outward constantly; the "most difficult puzzles ever devised" are finding challengers every day.

A Common Problem

Washington Redskins defensive linebacker Chris Draft had his first asthma attack while playing college football. He vividly remembers lying on the field struggling to breathe. Soon thereafter he was diagnosed with asthma. At first, he feared that the condition would prevent him from becoming a professional athlete. But with the help of his doctor, he learned how to manage his asthma. "I have to make sure I take my meds, and that I avoid triggers [substances that can provoke an asthma attack] like smoke and allergens,"[1] he explains.

Asthma is a chronic, or persistent, disease that affects a person's ability to breathe. Draft is just one of approximately 300 million people worldwide battling asthma. That breaks down to one in every twenty people.

In North America alone, approximately 10 percent of the population has asthma. About 20 million of these asthma sufferers live in the United States, and they are just the diagnosed cases. Healthcare professionals estimate that many more individuals have asthma but have not sought medical help or been diagnosed.

Asthmatics come from every walk of life: all races and ethnicities, male and female. Many are world-class athletes like Draft. More than nine million are children. In fact, asthma is the most common chronic disease in children throughout the world.

Of the twenty million asthma sufferers in the United States, over nine million are children.

Growing Numbers

Making matters worse, the number of new asthma cases is increasing rapidly. In 1990, about 10 million Americans were known to have asthma. That number doubled by 2010 and is projected to double again by 2025. Similar growth is projected throughout the world, including in developing nations. The rise of asthma in developing nations is especially troubling. Residents of developing nations often have limited access to medical care and asthma treatments. Since uncontrolled asthma can be fatal, lack of proper care is likely to cause a spike in asthma deaths. For example, the current death rate among Chinese asthma patients ages 5–34 exceeds 10 percent. In an address to the 61st World Health Organization's Assembly, Leslie Ramsammy of the World Health Organization (WHO) had this to say about the predicted rise in asthma cases and the danger it poses: "One of my colleagues, Sir George Alleyne, calls it the 'silent tsunami.' I have often referred to it as a festering sore."[2]

Taking a Toll

Because the incidence of asthma is so widespread, the condition has a substantial impact on individuals, families, and society, burdening the healthcare system, decreasing school and work productivity, and negatively affecting the quality of life of individuals with asthma and their families. People with asthma

A nurse administering a bronchodilator drug by nebulizer to an asthmatic infant. Asthma is the third leading cause of hospitalizations in American children.

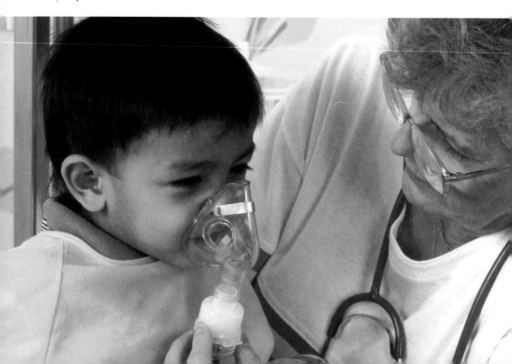

live with the stress of knowing that they can have an attack at any time. Approximately 35,000 Americans have an asthma attack every day. That adds up to about 12 million Americans a year. In the United States, an estimated 10 million visits to doctors' offices and emergency rooms annually are due to asthma. In fact, one out of every four emergency room visits is asthma related.

The disease causes 500,000 hospitalizations per year, with an average hospital stay of three days. It is the third leading cause of hospitalizations in American children. Kyle, a teen who has had asthma most of his life, explains: "I have been hospitalized four times over the past four years—for a week or more each time. I have also made many trips to the emergency room because I couldn't breathe and my puffers [asthma medication delivered through an inhaler] weren't helping."[3]

The cost of medical care combined with the cost of asthma medication comes to about 15 million dollars per year. And, although asthma is not usually life threatening, it can be. The disease kills about four thousand Americans annually, or about ten people a day.

Asthma also causes high rates of absenteeism in students and workers. American students miss a total of 13 million school days annually due to asthma. As a result, students can fall behind in their studies, teachers must reteach lessons, and parents are forced to miss work to stay home with sick children. Sarah Newman, a young woman with asthma, explains: "There were plenty of occasions where I couldn't go to school at all, and when you multiply this by the…children around the country with asthma, it adds up rather quickly. Teachers, nurses, principals and parents all bear the burden of the disease."[4]

The workplace is also impacted. American workers miss 25 million workdays annually due to asthma. In addition, some workers with asthma are forced to quit their jobs because of workplace exposure to substances that trigger their asthma symptoms.

Importance of Knowledge

There are ways, however, to lessen asthma's impact. By learning how to manage the disease, individuals with asthma can improve the quality of their lives. Utilizing such knowledge helps them to get their symptoms under control so that they can breathe more easily and lessens their risk of suffering a severe attack. This, in turn, helps reduce emergency room visits, hospitalizations, and school and workplace absenteeism. Three-time Olympic gold medal swimmer Nancy Hogshead explains: "I wish I had known about my asthma sooner, so I could have started feeling better sooner. Instead, I wasted a lot of time being frustrated when I got sick instead of knowing how to prevent getting sick altogether."[5]

And when friends, family, co-workers, teachers, and coaches learn more about asthma, they know how to provide asthmatics with appropriate support. In some cases, such support and knowledge can help keep asthma symptoms from escalating into a life-threatening asthma attack. Josh, a teen with asthma, explains: "Don't be afraid to let your teachers, your coaches, and your friends know about your asthma. If you are not feeling right, let someone know…. My friends don't treat me any differently because I have asthma, but they make sure that I'm alright. If I start wheezing, they check on me and tell me to calm down."[6]

CHAPTER ONE

Overly Sensitive Airways

Asthma is a disorder that affects a person's ability to breathe comfortably. The breathing tubes or airways of people with asthma are overly sensitive to any number of substances, events, or activities known as asthma triggers, which do not usually cause serious problems in other individuals. This sensitivity causes the immune systems of asthmatics to overreact. As a result, their airways become clogged and narrowed, which makes it difficult for air to move through them.

Asthma is a chronic condition. That means that once individuals develop it, and although their symptoms may come and go, they will almost always have asthma for the rest of their lives. At present, there is no cure for asthma, and scientists do not know for sure what causes it. Baltimore Ravens safety Haruki Nakamura, who was diagnosed with asthma when he was a toddler, explains: "I grew up my whole life with it. I'm a full-blown asthmatic. There's times when I spent weeks and weeks in the hospital, but I'm still here. I still made it to this point."[7]

The Airways

To understand asthma, it is necessary to look at the airways and how people breathe. The body depends on the airways, a roadlike network of about 100,000 tubes that looks like an upside-down tree, to carry air in and out of the lungs.

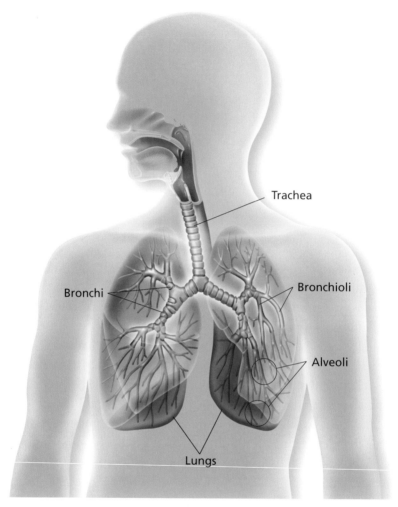

Anatomy of the airways, trachea, and lungs, with primary and secondary bronchi and bronchioli.

Normally, when people inhale, air is pushed from their mouth and nose down their throat to a long hollow tube known as the trachea or windpipe. It branches off into two smaller tubes called the bronchi, which connect to the right and left lungs. The bronchi branch off into thousands of smaller and smaller tubes within the lungs, known as bronchioles. They lead to millions of microscopic air sacs called alveoli, where oxygen and carbon dioxide are transferred in and out of the bloodstream. Carbon dioxide travels up the airways and out through the nose or mouth. Layers of muscles surround the airways.

If a person inhales a harmful substance, such as smoke from a burning building, the airways have natural defenses that protect the lungs. A thin layer of mucus covers their surface. Mucus is a sticky substance that traps harmful particles in much the same way flypaper traps insects. Tiny hairs called cilia that line the airways sweep the mucus up the airways, which relax and open wide so that the mucus can get through to the throat where it is coughed up and spat out or swallowed.

Dangerous Inflammation

The airways of a person with asthma, however, are hyperresponsive. That means they are overly sensitive to harmless substances and factors known as asthma triggers, such as allergens (substances like tree pollen that trigger an allergic reaction in people with allergies), air pollution, cold air, stress, and physical exercise. They respond to these triggers as if they posed a threat to the body. Instead of allowing mucus and cilia to get rid of the perceived threat, the body overreacts, signal-

A normal bronchus and an inflamed bronchus. The more inflammation that occurs, the more severe the asthma symptoms.

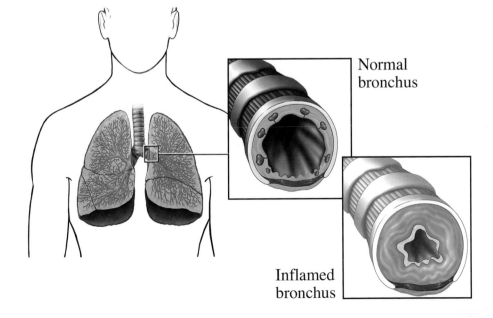

Normal
bronchus

Inflamed
bronchus

ing the immune system to launch an aggressive attack. As a result, powerful chemicals that cause inflammation, which is the body's chief method of fighting harmful organisms, are sent to the airways.

Ordinarily, inflammation is protective. It helps the body to fight off disease. Problems arise when inflammation does not shut down when a threat is eliminated or when it mistakenly attacks something harmless. In the case of asthma, since there is no actual threat to the body, rather than protecting the airways, inflammation sets off a dangerous chain of events. First, in an effort to get blood with infection-fighting white blood cells to the airways, inflammation causes the linings of the airways to swell. This makes the muscles surrounding the airways twitch, then tighten. As a result, the airways narrow, which makes it difficult for oxygen and carbon dioxide to pass through.

Inflammation also stimulates mucus production. Excess mucus forms sticky plugs that clog up the narrow airways, which makes it even harder to breathe. This causes the symptoms of asthma: coughing, which occurs as individuals try to expel the mucus plugs; wheezing, which is a whistling sound that is made as individuals try to push air through the airways; a burning sensation in the chest, which is caused by the narrowed airways; and difficulty breathing.

Depending on the level of inflammation at any given time, asthma symptoms can be so minor that individuals do not notice them or so severe that they can threaten lives—the greater the inflammation, the more severe the symptoms. "Inflammation," explains authors and asthma experts S. Hasan Arshad and K. Suresh Babu, "is the primary abnormality in asthma…everything else follows as a result of this."[8]

Complicating matters, once the airways become inflamed, they become even more sensitive. This sets off a dangerous inflammatory cycle in which the airways narrow and clog up more and more easily. As a result, even when people with asthma feel fine, there is always some inflammation in their airways. According to author and asthma expert William E. Berger,

This complex response can develop into a vicious cycle of worsening inflammation, hyperresponsiveness, constriction, and congestion, in which your airways become more and more sensitive and inflamed as a result of reacting to allergens, irritants, and other factors. The ongoing underlying airway inflammation is often so subtle that you don't notice it...[It] is like having a sunburn in your bronchial tubes.[9]

The Immune System

The immune system is the body's defense system against disease. It consists of billions of specialized cells that protect the body from harmful substances like bacteria, viruses, fungi, and parasites. When a foreign substance enters the body, the immune system sends white blood cells to the area. There are many types of white blood cells; each has a specific job.

Lymphocytes are the first cells that are released. When they come in contact with the invader, they engulf it. This causes bits of the foreign substance to stick to the lymphocytes. The composition of the foreign substance's protein alerts the immune system to the identity of the invader. If the substance is identified as an antigen—a harmful foreign substance—specialized proteins known as antibodies, each shaped to match up with and lock on to a specific antigen, are released. In the case of asthma, harmless substances such as pollen are mistaken for antigens.

Other white blood cells are also released during an immune response. Neutrophils are the most common. They attack bacteria. Dead neutrophils are what make up pus. Eosinophils and basophils are less common. Eosinophils attack parasites. Basophils are involved in causing inflammation.

An Asthma Attack

When inflammation gets out of control, the result is an asthma attack. During this attack, asthma symptoms escalate rapidly. The airways become so narrow and clogged that it takes a lot of effort to get air through them. The narrowed airways make exhaling difficult. As a result, carbon dioxide builds up in the body. Too much carbon dioxide can be deadly, which explains why the more carbon dioxide there is in a person's body, the greater their need to breathe. "Think about what happens if you turn on a spigot and there's a sharp bend in the hose…. The water can't get out of the hose, and stays bottled up at the point of obstruction. It's the same thing that happens when you have

A boy holding his chest during an asthma attack. Asthma is a disease in which the airways of the lungs become narrowed, which leads to shortness of breath, coughing, and wheezing.

decreased airflow through your ventilation [airways]," explains Dr. Mehmet Oz of New York Presbyterian Hospital. "Getting air out...feels like a vice is squeezing the bronchus [bronchi]."[10]

Making matters worse, excess carbon dioxide in the lungs and narrowed airways makes it difficult for oxygen to enter the body. Therefore, during an asthma attack, the person struggles to get air in and out of the body. This often makes the individual panic, which causes hyperventilation, or breathing too rapidly, further worsening asthma symptoms. People having an attack report feeling like they are slowly suffocating. If an attack is severe, lack of oxygen may turn victims' lips and fingertips blue and cause them to lose consciousness. The experience can be frightening. A teen with asthma explains:

> I have had asthma for a few years now and one day during softball practice I was having a great time with no problems at all...then I started coughing a bit, then it just started getting worse and more violent and I couldn't stop coughing enough to catch my breath and it went into a full blown attack...I was on the verge of passing out....[it was] very scary.[11]

Asthma Triggers

Any number of inhaled, ingested, injected, or touched substances, as well as physical activities and/or emotional factors, can set off the inflammatory process that causes an asthma attack. These are known as asthma triggers. Allergens, pollution, weather extremes, respiratory infections, chemicals (found in medicines, cleaning products, or perfumes), exercise, excitement, and stress are all examples of asthma triggers.

Allergens

Allergens are among the most common asthma triggers. Allergens are harmless substances like grass and tree pollens, dust mites, mold, and animal dander that cause the immune systems of people with allergies to overreact, setting off an inflamma-

Allergic asthma is asthma that is triggered by things such as grass, pollens, dust mites, mold, and animal dander.

tory reaction that can cause skin rashes, nasal congestion, and itchy eyes, among other symptoms.

Seventy percent of people with asthma also have allergies. Substances they are allergic to are common asthma triggers for them. Individuals whose asthma is triggered by allergens are said to have allergic asthma. Julia is one of these people. She is allergic to cat dander, microscopic flakes of an animal's skin that float around in the air and settle on objects like dust.

Exposure to it triggers her asthma symptoms. She explains: "I am allergic to cats and they trigger my asthma symptoms," she says. "When I'm close to them, my nose gets stuffed up and I start coughing. If I am not careful, the coughing escalates into an asthma attack."[12]

Nonallergen Triggers

Other triggers may not be allergy related. For example, smoke, which can be from tobacco products or from fires, and substances found in polluted air such as smog, vehicle exhaust fumes, chemicals, and particle matter, can also provoke an asthma attack in sensitive individuals. Gabby, a teen with asthma, describes how smoke affects her: "I was at softball practice …I began to smell smoke, like something was on fire. I continued with practice but the smoke smell got stronger. Then I started coughing…I kept coughing and coughing, really bad, and started wheezing…. Smoke is a trigger for my asthma."[13]

What are Allergies?

An allergy is a hypersensitivity disorder. Allergic individuals are overly sensitive to one or more allergens, normally harmless substances that do not cause problems in most other people. This sensitivity causes their immune system to overreact, setting off an inflammatory reaction. This makes people with allergies feel ill. Allergy symptoms may include nasal congestion, sneezing, coughing, watery eyes, headaches, itching, redness, hives, swelling, nausea, vomiting, diarrhea, and, when allergies provoke asthma, airway constriction. If allergy symptoms are severe and worsen rapidly, anaphylaxis can occur. It is a systematic response to allergens in a person's bloodstream. If it is not controlled, it causes a dangerous drop in blood pressure that can be fatal. Most people with allergies, however, do not experience anaphylaxis.

Salicylate, a chemical found in aspirin, triggers asthma symptoms in about 10 percent of all asthmatics. Other drugs can also be a trigger. Sulfites—food additives used to preserve beer, wine, dried fruit, and some processed foods—are another trigger. For unknown reasons, people with severe asthma are especially sensitive to sulfites.

Infections, which activate the immune system, also can trigger asthma symptoms in some people. In fact, the majority of asthma attacks in children are triggered by viral infections. According to Arshad and Babu, "The inflammation caused by infections makes the narrowing of the airways worse, leading to a flare-up."[14]

Extreme weather conditions, too, are common triggers. Cold dry air, for example, normally causes the airways to contract. Since the airways of people with asthma are chronically inflamed and not as relaxed as those of other people, anything that causes them to narrow further is not helpful. Abrupt weather changes, changes in humidity, and/or extreme changes in temperature, like walking from a warm heated building in winter into cold air, can also be a trigger. Emergency rooms report an increase in asthma cases during abrupt weather changes.

High humidity and electricity in the air during thunderstorms, and high winds, too, can affect some people with asthma. These weather conditions cause plants to release more pollens and mold spores, which trigger asthma attacks among asthmatics with pollen allergies. Stephen, whose symptoms are triggered by changes in humidity, explains:

I have always felt that changes in barometric pressure (which result in more or less rain and humidity and/or higher or lower temperatures) were a big factor in my asthma attacks…. If I go to bed on a clear night feeling fine then a high pressure system passes through while I am sleeping, I'll inevitably wake up during the night feeling constricted or with a full attack.[15]

Exercise-Induced Asthma

Physical exercise, which causes people to breathe harder and reduces heat and moisture in the airways, can also be a trigger in some people. Moisture in the lungs, which is normally replaced when people catch their breath, cannot be replaced in some people with asthma. Loss of moisture tightens the muscles around the airways.

Exercises that involve breathing cold dry air, like ice skating, snowboarding, and skiing, are especially problematic. Usually, people inhale cold air through the nose, where it is warmed and moistened before entering the airways. While exercising, individuals are more likely to breathe through their mouths. Cold air passes directly into the airways without the benefit

Asthmatics who enjoy cold weather sports, such as skiing or snowboarding, have to be extra careful of asthma attacks. The cold, dry air causes airways to contract, making it harder to breathe.

of being warmed and moistened in the nose, which can trigger an asthma attack. William Silver, of the University of Colorado and the Allergy, Asthma, and Immunology Clinic of Colorado, explains: "Very few asthmatics do well in cross country skiing because of the cold, dry air. You have a lot of heat loss and water loss from the airways, so you have a lot of asthma. There is a very high prevalence of asthma in cold air sports like cross country skiing."[16]

Multiple Triggers

Strong emotions, such as laughing or crying, are other triggers. Like physical exercise, they reduce moisture and heat in the airways and cause people to breathe harder, which makes the muscles around the airways tighten. Indeed, emotional stress, in general, can act as a trigger. It sets off and, in the case of asthmatics, worsens inflammation. According to health writer Sara Reistad-Long,

> In the basic human stress response, the hormones [chemicals] cortisol and adrenaline turn on the body's inflammatory system in order to get through the crisis. This may have worked well in ancient times when the stress had an endpoint, like outpacing a saber-toothed tiger. But now much of our anxiety, whether personal or professional, never goes away—and neither does the inflammation.[17]

Any number of these triggers can cause asthma symptoms in susceptible people. In fact, most asthmatics have multiple triggers. Mrs. Kazsa, the mother of two asthmatic children, Elyssa and Matthew, explains: "Elyssa's [asthma] seemed to mostly [flare] up after playing or laughing hard, or after being outdoors or in dusty/musty areas. Matthew showed signs of difficulty while around certain animals. They both had problems while they were sick and for some time afterwards as well."[18]

Who Gets Asthma?

Asthma triggers do not cause asthma; they induce asthma symptoms in people who already have the disease. Anyone can develop asthma, although some people are at greater risk than others.

Scientists do not know for sure what causes asthma, but they believe genetics plays a role. People with a family history of asthma are more likely to develop the condition than other individuals. This predisposition is passed down in a person's DNA from parent to child (DNA is the genetic material that determines the makeup of all cells). If a child has one parent with asthma, that child has a 25–50 percent chance of also having asthma. If both parents have asthma, that number increases somewhere between 51 and 80 percent. "As far as we know, nobody on my husband's side of the family has asthma," explains Mrs. Kazsa. "On my side, my mother and sister have it…. My doctor diagnosed me with mild asthma…. After almost one year of helping Matthew through his asthma…Elyssa was diagnosed with asthma around her two year birthday."[19]

The variation in the percentages is due to the fact that more than 100 genes appear to be involved with asthma. Inheriting any of these genes does not guarantee that individuals will develop asthma. Scientists believe that the more of these genes individuals inherit, the greater their susceptibility to developing asthma and the more severe the case.

Interestingly, some of these genes are more prevalent in African Americans than in other ethnic groups. This puts African Americans at a higher risk of developing asthma. According to the American Lung Association, the prevalence of asthma among African Americans is about 20 percent higher than in Caucasians. African Americans are also at risk of having a severe case of the disease. Three times as many African Americans are hospitalized and die from asthma than any other ethnic group in the United States.

Common Risk Factors

People with allergies, too, are at risk of developing asthma. Like asthma, allergies run in families and have a genetic link. Some people with asthma, however, do not have allergies or a family history of allergies or asthma. This group includes people in professions who are exposed to irritating chemicals on a regular basis. Scientists have identified more than three hundred different workplace irritants, including chemical fumes, dust, smoke, gases, animal substances, and metals, among others. Regularly inhaling large amounts of any of these irritants can weaken and irritate the airways and can cause people to develop an allergy to the substance. Scientists think that such factors make these individuals more susceptible to developing asthma. On the other hand, an estimated 11 million American workers are regularly exposed to at least one of these substances, but not all of them develop asthma. Scientists do not know why this is so.

According to the U.S. Department of Labor, about 15 percent of all adult asthma cases may be linked to work-related factors.

People can develop asthma from exposure to factors in the workplace. Firefighters are regularly exposed to smoke, soot, and dust and have the third highest rate of occupational asthma.

Professions that are hardest hit include firefighters, dry cleaners, textile workers, bakers, hairdressers, painters, construction workers, janitors, and certain factory workers who inhale harmful chemicals on the job. Firefighters, for instance, are regularly exposed to smoke, soot, dust, and smoldering wood chips, among other irritants. A three-year California study that ended in 2009 found that firefighters reported the third highest rate of occupational asthma after janitors and dry cleaners, who are exposed to a wide variety of chemical fumes from cleaning agents on a daily basis. Coincidentally, a 2010 study conducted by the Center for Research in Environmental Epidemiology in Barcelona, Spain, found that breathing in bleach, ammonia, and stain removers more than once a week was linked with a 20 percent rise in asthma.

Workers in other fields, too, can be affected by cleaning products. Marcel worked in a dairy for more than seventeen years, where he inhaled a chemical mist from a cleaning product that was used to sanitize feeding machines. "My first clue was coughing and wheezing that wouldn't go away," he explains. "I didn't have asthma as a child and I never smoked. So I went to see my doctor.... For years I had been breathing in that chemical mist.... After a lot of tests and examinations, my doctor diagnosed occupational asthma."[20]

Likewise, painters and factory workers in plants that deal with chemicals known as isocynates are at high risk. These workers often wear special masks to help minimize irritation to their lungs. However, isocynates are so irritating to the lungs that even slight exposure can cause asthma to develop in some people, but not in everyone. Once again, scientists do not know why this is so.

There is still a lot to learn about asthma. It is clear that a number of factors determine who develops the condition, and that a wide variety of substances can trigger asthma symptoms. The resultant inflammation produces a number of symptoms, which, without proper treatment, can be dangerous.

CHAPTER TWO

Diagnosis and Treatments

When patients complain of recurrent episodes of coughing, wheezing, tightness in the chest, and/or shortness of breath, doctors suspect asthma. Diagnosis involves an examination and medical tests. Once a diagnosis is made, the severity of the case is assessed. Then, treatment begins. It usually involves the use of two types of medications. One provides quick relief during an asthma attack, and the other helps manage inflammation so that asthma symptoms are less likely to flare up.

The Physical Examination

Asthma is not the only disease characterized by coughing, wheezing, tightness in the chest, and shortness of breath. Respiratory infections, lung cancer, and some forms of heart disease and acid reflux, a digestive disorder, also share these symptoms. Medical professionals must eliminate these other conditions before making a diagnosis of asthma. Carefully questioning patients, learning their medical history, and administering a physical examination helps healthcare professionals make an accurate diagnosis.

First, patients are asked to describe their symptoms and whether the symptoms appeared suddenly, as in the case of an infection; are seasonal; are constant; or occur after exposure to certain substances or factors. Questions about whether the patient has allergies, as well as the patient's family and work history, are also important. Having allergies, a family history of asthma, or regular exposure to certain irritants in the workplace put patients at high risk of developing asthma.

A physical examination is administered next. Although the exam focuses on the lungs and airways, the doctor will also check for nasal discharge and swelling, which are signs of allergies or infections. A chest x-ray may also be administered. This gives a clearer picture of the lungs and can help rule out lung cancer.

Inflamed airways react to asthma triggers by narrowing and producing excess mucus. Healthcare proffessionals are able to see and diagnose these respiratory symptoms by administering a chest x-ray during a physical exam.

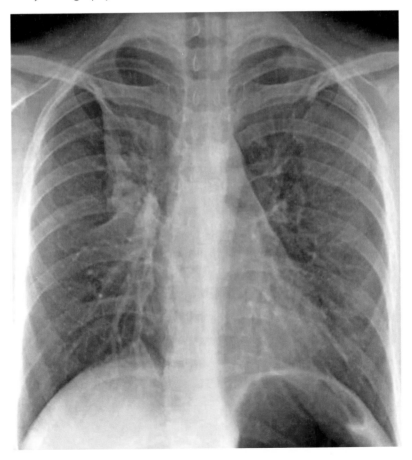

Measuring Lung Function

Next, a spirometry test is administered. It measures how well the lungs are functioning, or the lung function value. During the test, patients blow as hard as they can into a tube-like device that is attached to a computer. The computer measures the amount and speed of the air that the patient exhales. The measurement is compared to normal airflow for a person of the same age, gender, height, and race as established by the American Thoracic Society. If the airflow is less than normal, the patient is treated with a bronchodilator, which is a quick-acting asthma relief medication that opens up the airways. Then the patient is retested. If the patient's airflow increases significantly, this is evidence of asthma. If it does not, asthma is ruled out. According to Arshad and Babu, "An improvement in spirometry results…following treatment, is a cornerstone of the diagnosis of asthma."[21]

A young girl undergoes a spirometry test to measure how well her lungs are functioning.

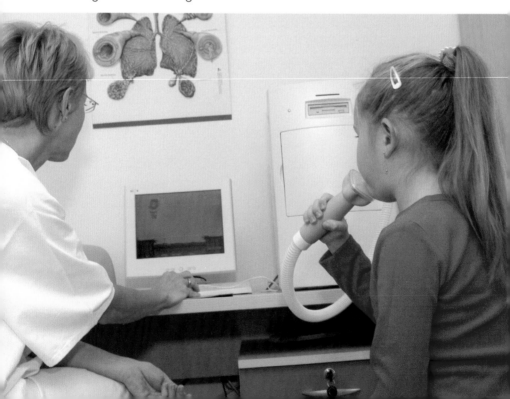

Swimmer Nancy Hogshead did not suspect she had asthma, but a spirometry test indicated she did. She explains:

The first time a doctor asked me to...test for asthma, I thought he was crazy. I thought people with asthma were sickly wheezers. I was a world champion swimmer.... Sure I was sick a lot and tended to cough during and after working out, but who doesn't breathe hard after an intense match.... But the doctor told me... approximately 10 percent of Olympic athletes from all over the world have asthma. He then gave me a list of the symptoms and I had all of them.... I agreed to the test, and was astonished to discover that when I really pushed it, I could be swimming with 40% decrease in my lung capacity![22]

Assessing the Severity

Once a diagnosis of asthma is made, its severity is established. This helps medical professionals determine the best treatment for the patient. The goal of treatment is to control asthma symptoms, reduce the frequency and severity of asthma attacks, and relieve airway obstruction. Because different cases of asthma require different treatment, with the most severe cases requiring the most powerful medication, healthcare professionals evaluate the severity of the patient's symptoms in order to prescribe the most effective treatment. To simplify the process, the National Institute of Health has established four stages of asthma based on the frequency of the patient's symptoms and the patient's lung function value.

These four stages are classified as mild intermittent, mild persistent, moderate persistent, and severe persistent. Mild intermittent asthma is the least severe type. Symptoms occur less than twice a week and lung function is normal between flare-ups. Although lung function remains normal between flare-ups in mild persistent asthma, symptoms occur more than twice a week but not daily, making it more troublesome. In moderate persistent asthma, symptoms occur daily and lung function is below normal even between flare-ups. Symptoms in severe persistent asthma occur almost continuously and lung function is always below normal. The regularity of symptoms in moderate persistent and severe persistent asthma can limit a patient's physical activity and quality of their life.

The Stepwise Approach to Treatment

Once the severity of the patient's asthma is determined, treatment begins. However, asthma stages are not permanent. A patient's classification can go up or down depending on how well the disease is controlled. At the start of treatment, healthcare professionals work to lower the patient's classification using the stepwise approach to treatment. According to asthma expert Berger, "The basic concept of stepwise management is to initially prescribe long-term and quick-relief medications, based on the severity level that's one step higher than the severity level you're experiencing."[23]

For instance, patients diagnosed with mild intermittent asthma are initially treated as if they have mild persistent asthma. Those with mild persistent asthma are treated as if they have moderate persistent asthma, and so on.

This approach has proven to be effective in rapidly reducing asthma symptoms. Once the patient's symptoms are controlled for at least a month, the medication is reduced, or stepped down, by one level. Patients usually remain on this stepped-down level of medication for the long term. "Using the stepwise approach to asthma management means that you step up your medication therapy to gain control, and then step down to maintain control,"[24] Berger explains.

Inhaled Medication

There are many different medications used to treat asthma. These medicines can be delivered in the form of liquid, pill, or capsule, but the most common method is through an inhaler. An inhaler is a small handheld device that converts a measured dose of liquid or powdered medication into a mist or a fine powder, which is sprayed through the mouth and inhaled

Although asthma medication can be delivered in pill, capsul, powder or liquid form, the most common method of delivery is by inhaler.

into the airways. There are many different types of inhalers. The most common look like a little spray can with a nozzle on one end, where medication mists out, and an instrument called a spacer on the other end, which holds the medication until patients breathe it into their lungs.

Inhalers have many advantages over oral medication in treating asthma. They are small and fairly easy to use. Individuals can carry them in their pockets or purses. And, they deliver a high concentration of medication directly into the airways quickly, which means less medicine is needed to provide fast relief. "Inhalers," explain Arshad and Babu, "enable people with asthma to lead active lives without fear of an attack. This is because inhalers are portable and convenient, and can provide immediate relief."[25]

When Using an Inhaler is Not Possible

Although an inhaler is relatively easy to use, individuals must be able to hold the inhaler, release the spray, and inhale the medication all at the same time. Babies, young children, and the elderly may not be able to do so. They often use a nebulizer instead. It is an air compressor or ultrasonic machine that discharges an easy-to-inhale mist of asthma medication into a patient's airways through a facemask or mouthpiece connected to the device by plastic tubing. Using a nebulizer requires very little effort from the patient. And, larger doses of asthma medication can be delivered via nebulizer than via an inhaler, which is why nebulizers are often used in hospitals to treat severe asthma attacks. According to Arshad and Babu,

> A slight disadvantage of inhalers is that some effort is required for effective use and that the dose delivered with one puff is relatively small. In an exacerbation [a severe attack], when large doses are needed by a patient who is breathless, it may not be possible to inhale the required dose effectively. In these situations, a...nebulizer is used to deliver the bronchodilator [asthma rescue medicine] in a mist form.[26]

An asthma patient breathing into a nebulizer. A nebulizer is easier for patients to use than an inhaler and can offer higher doses of medication.

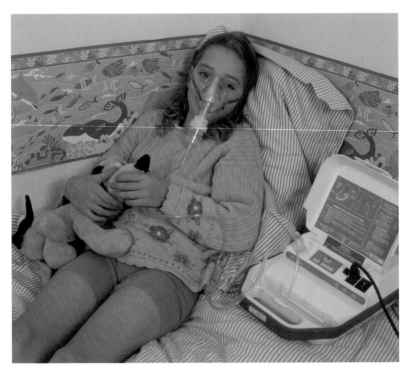

Nebulizers come in different sizes and can be powered by electricity or batteries. Treatment delivered with a nebulizer usually takes ten to fifteen minutes.

Rescue Medicine

There are two types of asthma medication: quick relief, or rescue, medicine and preventive medicine. Both are usually delivered via an inhaler or nebulizer and both are important in managing asthma.

Quick-relief medications, which are also known as short-acting bronchodilators, are rescue drugs that are used to provide fast, temporary relief from asthma symptoms. They help to stop asthma attacks both when symptoms threaten and after an attack has started. Short-acting bronchodiators are not taken daily but rather are used on an as-needed basis to ease asthma symptoms.

There are different classes of drugs that serve as bronchodilators. Those most commonly prescribed for asthma are called beta-agonists. Beta-agonists work like adrenaline, a chemical the body produces naturally in times of crisis. Beta-agonists help the body respond quickly to an emergency by raising the patient's heart rate and blood pressure and relaxing the airways. Chemicals in these drugs attach to and stimulate cells called beta-receptors located in the small muscles surrounding the airways. Stimulating beta-receptors causes the muscles to relax and the airways to open, which allows asthmatics to breathe easier.

Short-acting bronchodilators are fast acting. They take effect in about five minutes and keep working for about one hour. Although they open the airways, they have no effect on the underlying inflammation. In addition, bronchodilators, like any other drug, can cause negative side effects such as high blood pressure, a rapid heartbeat, muscle pain and cramps, nervousness, and/or wakefulness.

However, because quick-relief medication can save an asthmatic's life, the benefit of the medication exceeds the health risks. Asthmatics are advised to carry an inhaler containing rescue medicine with them at all times. John-Henry, a teenager with asthma, explains:

> The first time I had to take care of an asthma attack was when I signed up for soccer team. My dad was the coach, but didn't have the constant time to help me when I had an attack or needed my medications. I was a goalie and while I was trying to hold the goal from balls getting kicked in, I was also struggling to breathe! Yes, I was allergic to grass, sagebrush, you name it and it was all happening at once! I realized then that I needed to take care of myself and carry my medication with me. It was neat too: I remember working with my parents to drill holes in the plastic holder [of the inhaler] and put a string around it and I knew that my medicine would be with me always![27]

Having immediate access to the drug is so vital that, although most schools require students to store medications with the school nurse who administers the drugs as needed, when it comes to asthma quick-relief medication, this is not the case. Right-to-carry asthma rescue medicine laws have been passed throughout the United States. These laws permit asthmatic students to carry their inhalers with them at all times and to self-administer the medication as needed. South Dakota became the last state to pass this law in 2010. South Dakota respiratory therapist and asthma educator Rae O' Leary explains: "Before this, it was only a matter of time until a student took their last breath because of a delayed response to medication at school. That clock has now stopped ticking for students… with asthma…because they will no longer have to wait for life-saving medication during an attack."[28]

Preventive Medicine

Unlike quick-relief medicine, preventive or long-term control medicine is taken regularly even when patients do not have any asthma symptoms. Preventive medications are anti-inflammatory drugs. That means they interfere with the immune system

Having a rescue medicine inhaler available is so vital to asthmatics that right-to-carry laws have been passed in the U.S. to allow students who have asthma to carry their inhalers with them at all times.

by reducing inflammation, a chronic problem in people with asthma. By controlling inflammation, preventive medicine reduces the possibility of an asthma flare-up, but it has no effect on the airways once an attack is in progress.

There are a number of different preventive medicines. The most popular are corticosteroids. This medicine contains cortisol, man-made copies of inflammation-fighting steroids or hormones found in the human body. Corticosteroids are powerful drugs that suppress the immune system. In so doing, they decrease swelling, mucus production, and hyperresponsiveness in the airways. And, since the drug helps keep the airways

Alternative Asthma Treatments

Alternative treatments are treatments that are not widely accepted by the traditional medical community in the United States. Unlike conventional treatments, alternative treatments are not subject to rigorous testing and careful regulation by the Federal Drug Administration (FDA).

Despite this, many asthma patients add alternative treatments to traditional asthma treatments in an effort to better control their symptoms. The Buteyko method is one such treatment. It teaches people with asthma to change their breathing patterns in order to prevent them from breathing too rapidly, which can worsen asthma symptoms. Patients learn to breathe through the nose rather than the mouth and to suppress the urge to gasp for air.

Acupuncture is also popular. Acupuncturists insert hair-thin needles into specific points in the patient's body in an effort to open the flow of energy within the body. This, acupuncturists say, helps the immune system function better, resulting in a reduction in lung hyperresponsiveness, decreased mucus production, and relaxed airways.

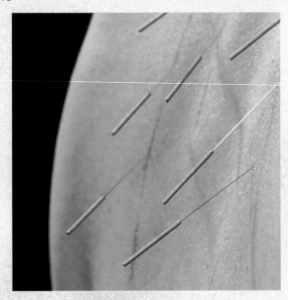

Acupuncture is used by some as an alternative treatment for asthma.

open, when an attack does threaten, consistent use of preventive medication keeps the airways from tightening as severely.

In contrast to rescue medicine, preventive medicine does not work immediately. It must build up in an individual's bloodstream before taking effect. Patients must use the medication consistently for about two weeks before they see any improvement in their symptoms. Although it is possible to lessen the dosage once patients have few or no symptoms, this is best undertaken under the supervision of a medical professional. Some people think that once their asthma symptoms are gone, they can stop taking preventive medication entirely. This is a mistake. Doing so erases the medicine's protective effect. As a consequence, if patients stop using their long-term controller medicine, their asthma symptoms will gradually worsen, which often results in a severe asthma attack. Author and asthma expert Thomas F. Plaut puts it this way: "When it rains, an umbrella can keep you dry. Do you close it while it is still raining? No. You will get wet. Asthma 'control' medicines work like an umbrella. They protect you from asthma symptoms and episodes. Symptoms often return when you stop taking long-term control medicine."[29]

Because preventive asthma medicine is inhaled, only small amounts enter the bloodstream. Therefore, the medication does not present the same health risk as ingested or injected steroids, which can weaken the bones, damage the heart, and cause muscle weakness. In fact, the bad effects of inhaling a daily dose of corticosteroids is less than that of taking an oral steroid every day for two weeks. However, since steroids suppress the immune system, long-term controller medicine can affect a person's health. Individuals may suffer from infections, such as the flu or pneumonia, but their immune system will not react as aggressively as it would without the presence of steroids. Therefore, individuals may not exhibit symptoms like fever early on, and they may not know they are sick until the infection becomes severe. In addition, if a person uses the inhaler incorrectly and corticosteroids are sprayed onto the throat instead of the airways, steroids build up in the throat and a fungus forms. This can cause an unpleasant fungal infection known as thrush, which causes a sore throat.

On the other hand, by reducing asthma symptoms, long-term controller medicine can greatly improve asthma sufferers' quality of life. "I take my medicine everyday," Julia says. "Since I started using it everyday, I have not had an asthma attack. It's been a couple of years. I don't like taking medicine, but I am afraid not to take my preventive medicine. It has really helped me."[30]

Long-term Bronchodilators
Sometimes corticosteroids are not enough to control an individual's asthma symptoms, especially in cases of severe persistent asthma. In these cases, corticosteroids are combined with another drug, a long-term bronchodilator, in an effort to

Salt Therapy

Some people with asthma are visiting former salt caves in Eastern Europe and Asia and synthetic salt caves in Great Britain to ease asthma symptoms. These caves have been turned into clinics for people with asthma and other respiratory illnesses. The clinics claim that inhaling tiny antibacterial salt particles in a sterile atmosphere helps loosen mucus plugs and unblock the airways. This type of therapy has been practiced in Eastern Europe since the early nineteenth century when scientists noted that workers in local salt mines rarely had respiratory illnesses.

The clinics are located underground. All the walls and ceilings are made of salt. There are rooms with beds, and a lounge area. Patients spend their days in the clinic breathing in the salt air and nights in a nearby hospital. Treatment usually lasts about ten days.

There is no proof that breathing in salt can relieve asthma symptoms, although many patients say it has helped them. Any relief the therapy gives is temporary. It cannot cure asthma.

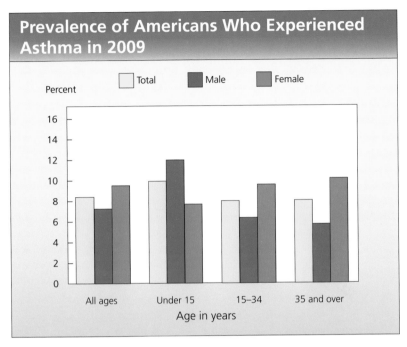

Prevalence of Americans Who Experienced Asthma in 2009

DATA SOURCE: CDC/HCHS, National Health Interview Survey, 2009, combined Sample Adult and Sample Child Core components. www.cdc.gov/nchs/data/nhis/earlyrelease/201006_15.pdf.

control asthma symptoms. In fact, some drug manufacturers have combined the two medications in one inhaler to make it easier for patients who need them. Over time, the combination of the two medications has been known to get asthma symptoms under such good control that patients can step down and discontinue the long-term bronchodilator.

Long-term bronchodilators work like short-term bronchodilators. They relax and open the muscles surrounding the airways. But, rather than taking effect immediately, long-term bronchodilators take at least thirty minutes to take effect and last for twelve hours.

Long-term bronchodilators are not without risk. The medicine has been associated with severe asthma attacks and asthma deaths, especially when the drug is taken without an inhaled steroid. A twenty-eight week 2006 U.S. study known as the Salmeterol Multi-Center Asthma Research Trial, or SMART,

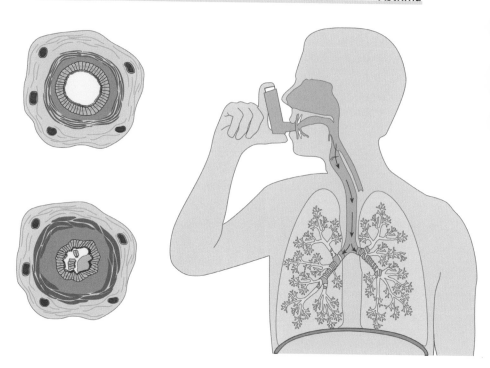

Bronchodilator drugs work by widening the airways (the bronchioles) of the lungs (upper left). During an asthma attack, bronchioles become narrow following contraction of the muscle layer and swelling of the mucous lining (lower left). This leads to impaired breathing.

compared the safety of long-term bronchodilators on 13,176 asthmatics to a placebo, or sugar pill, on an equal number of asthmatics. Subjects in both groups who used inhaled steroid medication before entering the study continued to do so. There were thirteen asthma-related deaths among the subjects using the long-term bronchodilator, compared to three asthma-related deaths in the placebo group. The study did not attempt to prove whether using inhaled corticosteroids in conjunction with a long-term bronchodilator made a difference in the results. However, the researchers observed that hospitalizations and severe asthma symptoms were reduced when the two drugs were used together. It is not clear why this is so, but it appears that daily use of long-term bronchodilators without corticosteroids, which control inflammation, can cause patients to miss signs of worsening inflammation. By the time patients realize there is a problem, asthma symptoms may be out of control. Because of these results, in 2010 the U.S. Food and Drug Administration (FDA), the government agency that regulates all prescription and nonprescription drugs sold in the United States, required that manufacturers of long-term bronchodilators place a warning on the package that alerts patients not to use the drug without inhaled steroids. It also alerts them to the fact that long-term bronchodilators have been linked to potential safety risks, but the risk is not strong enough to remove the drug from the market. Knowing this, patients and doctors can make informed decisions about using the medication. According to Allergy and Asthma Network Mothers of Asthmatics (AANMA) board chairman and noted asthma expert Stuart Stoloff, "The determination of safety of any medicine is based on the risk/benefit ratio and should be discussed between the physician/clinician and the patient."[31]

Because of the benefits, many patients with severe asthma are willing to take the risk. According to Nancy Sanders, founder and president of the AANMA: "When prescribed and used as a comprehensive treatment plan, 12 hour bronchodilators have given back to patients the ability to work, climb stairs, attend school, sleep through the night, and compete in sports without symptoms—things most others take for granted."[32]

Clearly, like all medications, those used to treat asthma can have harmful side effects. Yet, despite the problems that asthma medications can cause, most healthcare professionals and people with asthma agree that effectively using rescue and preventive medications is a major step in controlling asthma symptoms, and that these medications can save lives.

CHAPTER THREE

Managing Asthma Triggers

Regularly taking preventive asthma medication is an important step in reducing inflammation in the airways, which helps reduce asthma symptoms. Identifying and minimizing exposure to asthma triggers is also essential in controlling asthma. Although this is not always easy, doing so can significantly lessen an individual's asthma symptoms and the risk of an asthma attack. Berger explains:

> Avoidance seems simple enough. In real life, however, the trick is figuring out—short of living in a bubble—the practical and effective steps you can take to minimize your contact with triggers. Environmental control measures are vital components of any...treatment plan. Every practicing allergist [doctor who treats allergies and allergy related asthma] focuses on helping you create and implement an effective avoidance strategy for you, your spouse, your child, or other people with asthma who live with you.[33]

Identifying Triggers

A major step in controlling asthma is identifying what substances, events, or factors trigger an individual's symptoms. Once this is known, asthmatics can take steps to avoid or limit their exposure to these triggers. When this is not possible, they can take medication that desensitizes their immune system to the triggers and/or use asthma rescue medication before and after being exposed to the triggers. Since most individuals with asthma are sensitive to multiple triggers, identifying all of them is not easy. Keeping an asthma diary can help. In it, individuals record how they feel every day. They note their general health, asthma symptoms, and emotional state. They include specific information such as where they went, what the weather was, whom they were with, what activities they participated in, and what, if any, effect these factors had on their asthma symptoms. Individuals and healthcare professionals use this information to analyze what factors encourage or worsen a patient's asthma symptoms and to pinpoint specific triggers. For instance, if patients note that they cough and wheeze on cold days, this indicates that their airways are sensitive to cold air. Knowing this, they can then take steps to minimize their exposure to

Asthmatics can help identify their triggers by keeping an asthma diary. In it, individuals can record how they feel every day, including general health, asthma symptoms, and emotional state.

Pollen Counts

Many people with asthma are sensitive to pollen. Checking the daily pollen count and taking steps to limit outdoor activities when pollen counts are high can help individuals who are sensitive to pollen manage their symptoms. Most newspapers report the local pollen count everyday. It is a measurement of the total number of pollen grains found in each cubic meter of air. The count is for all types of pollens and is not usually broken down into particle types.

Pollen counts fall into five categories: no pollen; low, or 1-10 pollen grains per cubic meter; moderate, or 11 to 50 pollen grains per cubic meter; high, or 51 to 500 pollen grains per cubic meter; and very high, or more than 500 pollen grains per cubic meter. Most asthmatics who are sensitive to pollen experience asthma symptoms on high and very high pollen days. Moderate and low days affect only the most sensitive individuals.

A heavy rain can lower the pollen count, while wind and a brief thunderstorm can spread pollen.

The common ragweed pollen is highly allergenic, as the greatest pollen allergen of all pollens.

cold air. In this manner, individuals gain more control over their asthma.

Allergy Tests

If patients note in their asthma diary that their symptoms are seasonal, or that they worsen when they are outdoors, or when

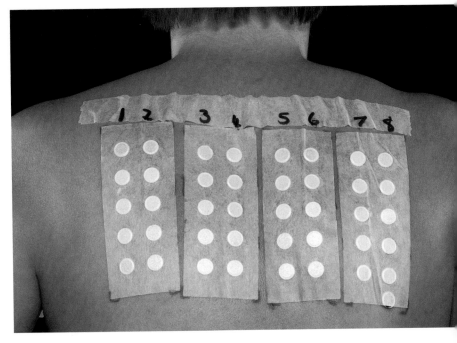

A person being tested for allergies.

they are around dust, mold, or pets, it is likely that allergens trigger their symptoms. Since most people with allergies are sensitive to multiple substances, undergoing an allergy test is a way to help identify exactly what allergens trigger asthma symptoms in affected individuals.

The most common test is a skin prick or scratch test. It involves exposing the skin to different allergens and then observing the body's reaction. During the test, a healthcare professional applies small drops of diluted extracts of different allergens to tiny scratches on the patient's forearm or back. As many as seventy allergens may be applied during one test and may include various plant and tree pollen, dust, mold, and pet dander.

If the patient is sensitive to a particular allergen, the skin where the allergen was applied will become red and swollen. This indicates that inflammation is present, which means the body is having an allergic reaction to the particular allergen.

This does not conclusively prove that the allergen is an asthma trigger, but in most cases when an asthmatic's skin is sensitive to a particular allergen, so too are their airways. This was the case for former NFL defensive linebacker Chad Brown, who developed asthma symptoms when he moved to Seattle. He recalls: "I couldn't figure out what had happened to me. I was a great player in Pittsburgh and then I come to Seattle and suddenly I can't breathe. I'd done the exact same type of workouts in the off-season to maintain my shape. So it's just simply the allergens in the air in Seattle."[34]

Avoiding Household Triggers

Once individuals know their triggers, whether they are allergens or nonallergens, they can take steps to minimize their exposure to them.

Many asthma triggers, such as dust mites, mold, cockroach droppings, mice, secondhand smoke, and fumes from household cleansers, can be found around the house. Dust mites, in particular, are one of the most common of all asthma triggers. An estimated 75 percent of individuals with allergic asthma are sensitive to them.

Dust mites are microscopic spider-like creatures that thrive in any dark, warm, moist environment. They live in dust, feeding on dead skin flakes, which humans shed. Since humans shed lots of dead skin as they sleep, the bedroom is a popular home for dust mites. In fact, the average bed contains about two million of them. As much as 10 percent of the weight of an old pillow is made up of dust mites, their droppings, and human skin, which is one reason why many individuals' asthma symptoms worsen at night. Dust mites also can be found in stuffed toys, upholstered furniture, rugs, and curtains.

It is impossible to totally avoid the little creatures, but individuals can reduce their exposure to them by encasing their bedding in special covers that repel dust mites. They can wash their bedding and stuffed toys in hot water, put stuffed toys in the freezer for about five hours each week to kill the mites, keep stuffed toys off their beds, and use an air conditioner or a dehumidifier to dry out household air, which makes it more difficult for dust mites to survive. Vacuuming carpets and cloth-covered furniture with a vacuum that has a high efficiency particle arrester (HEPA) filter, an air filtration device that filters out tiny particles like dust mites, also helps. According to Berger, "HEPA filters absorb and contain 99.97 percent of all particles larger than 0.3 microns (1/300 the width of a human hair)…HEPA filters are vital tools for desensitizing and allergy proofing your indoor environment."[35] However, since any vacuum briefly increases the amount of dust mites in the air, it is best if someone who does not have asthma vacuums and that individuals with asthma leave the room during the process.

In an effort to completely dislodge dust mites, some asthmatics get rid of all curtains, soft upholstered furniture, and rugs, replacing them with roll shades or mini-blinds, leather, vinyl, or wood furniture, and hard flooring. Sarah, a woman with asthma explains: "I hate carpet!…A night in a carpeted room for me is a

A close up of a house dust mite. Millions of dust mites inhabit the home, feeding on shed skin cells. They mainly live in furniture and carpet, and are usually harmless. However, their excrement and dead bodies may cause allergic reactions in those with asthma.

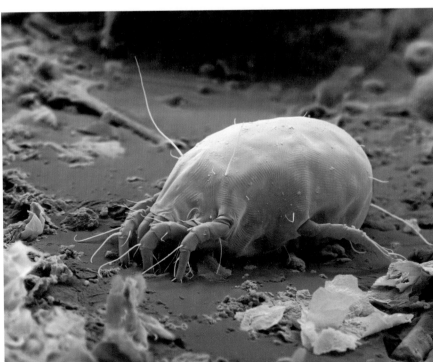

sleepless night...It's to the point that I've decided I shall never live in a house or apartment with carpeting."[36]

Mold Indoors and Outdoors

Mold is another common household trigger that is often linked to carpeting. Like dust mites, mold needs humidity to flourish. If carpets get wet, the padding underneath can retain mold. It also thrives in bathrooms, laundry areas, basements, attics, refrigerators, houseplants, garbage cans, and other damp parts of the house. Mold is found outdoors, too. The spores typically increase on humid, rainy, and foggy days and can get into the house through open windows, doors, and vents.

Approximately one in four asthmatics is sensitive to mold. In fact, a 2010 study that examined the effect of mold on children with asthma in New Orleans after Hurricane Katrina found a rise in asthma symptoms among asthmatic children because of the increased concentration of mold throughout the city. Researcher Floyd Malveauz explains:

The mold concentration increased tremendously—in homes and throughout the indoor and outdoor environment. Many children left the area...Those who did stay, we worked with them and tested them. We found about 78 percent of those who had asthma were sensitive to mold....If you're in an environment that's quite humid like New Orleans, there is already a lot of mold in the air. With the flooding, when there was up to eight to ten feet of water, you're creating a very moist environment. It becomes a big soup where microorganisms grow. The mold remains in the walls, carpeting, and just takes over the environment.[37]

Keeping home humidity below 50 percent helps eliminate mold. Using an air purifier with a HEPA filter also helps. An air purifier is a machine that helps clean indoor air and can filter out mold and other irritants. Getting rid of houseplants that harbor mold in the soil, as well as cleaning such damp areas as bathrooms, washing machines, trash cans, walls, floors, and ceilings with bleach or other mold-killing solutions, also reduces its presence. However, chemicals and scents in household cleansers trigger asthma symptoms in some individuals. For this reason, many asthmatics substitute homemade cleansers that combine baking soda, vinegar, or lemon juice with water for those products with irritating chemicals. They also use unscented detergents, soaps, and beauty products.

Other Household Triggers

Other household triggers can also be minimized. Exposure to secondhand smoke can be eliminated when asthmatics ban smoking from their homes. This often means that family members of asthmatic children have to give up smoking. Ketan Sheth of the Lafayette Allergy and Asthma Clinic in Indiana, explains: "The biggest thing people need to think about is not smoking

Asthmatic children whose parents smoke are more likely to have asthma attacks, as secondhand smoke is a trigger for sensitive individuals.

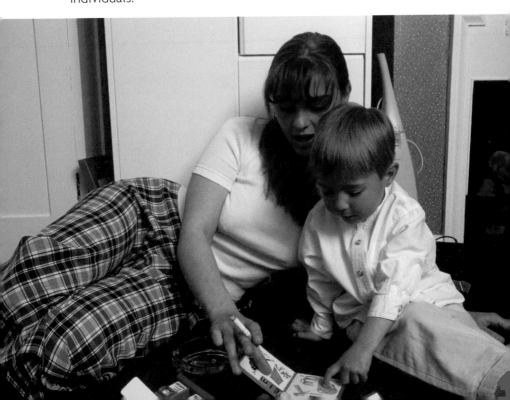

around their child. This means don't smoke at home around your child; don't smoke with your child in the car. People can carry the smoke on their clothes."[38] Smoke from fireplaces and woodstoves can also be a problem for sensitive individuals. The easiest way to solve it is by not having a fire in the house.

Other triggers such as cockroach droppings are harder to control. The bugs are a particular problem in urban areas, where people live in apartments and row houses where the creatures can move freely through the connecting walls. An estimated three-quarters of all urban homes in the United States have cockroaches, and it is not uncommon for homes to be infested with thousands of the insects. Some asthma experts theorize that this is one reason asthma is especially common in American inner cities.

To minimize cockroach droppings, asthma patients are advised to keep their kitchens free of crumbs and wash out pet bowls and dirty dishes. Many individuals hire a pest control professional to destroy cockroaches in their home. As a final step, they seal cracks in their walls to eliminate cockroach entry points. Sealing holes and cracks also helps minimize an infestation of mice, whose droppings can also trigger asthma symptoms in susceptible people.

Problems with Pets

Other nonhuman household members are more welcome. Many households include pets, and although they are often beloved family members, they trigger asthma symptoms in about 30 percent of asthmatics. Even though giving up a pet can be very difficult, many people with asthma do this in order to lessen their asthma symptoms. Rachel Aydt gave her cat away when she learned cat dander was triggering the asthma symptoms of her young son, Jamie. "For Jamie, sacrificing his breathing wasn't an option…. After a trip to the emergency room, we made the agonizing decision to send Charlie [the cat] away. To date, this is the biggest parental sacrifice I've ever made,"[39] she explains.

Asthmatics who choose to keep their pets often keep them outdoors as much as possible. When they are allowed indoors, they sometimes are kept in a restricted area. That is what Julia, whose asthma is triggered by cat dander, did with her cat. She explains: "I kept him out of my bedroom and off all the furniture. It didn't keep me from having problems, but it helped somewhat."[40]

Some asthmatics alter their social life in order to minimize their exposure to animal dander. They avoid visiting friends and family members who have pets, opting to meet somewhere else instead, which is what Matt does. He explains:

> If I spend any more than 10-15 minutes in a house with even one cat...I'm doomed....I...need to use my rescue inhaler 3 to 4 times as often as I usually do...It becomes a social issue at some point....I've had to pass up potentially good relationships over animals. I've inadvertently hurt feelings because of them. I don't get asked to friends' houses who I've told about the problem. Now, I still have a great social life with many friends, but we go out, or they come to my house.[41]

Managing Outdoor Triggers

Avoiding exposure to outdoor triggers like pollens, air pollution, and certain weather conditions is almost impossible. But individuals can still take actions that help. People who are sensitive to pollen or air pollution can avoid outdoor activity on high pollen or ozone alert days. Staying indoors in the early morning and late afternoon hours when pollen counts are typically highest also helps. It also helps to keep doors and windows closed and use a clothes dryer rather than hanging wet clothes outside where they trap pollen. Wearing a filter mask when working outdoors is another strategy. Doing so helps filter out air pollution and pollens. Similarly, for those individuals whose asthma symptoms are triggered by cold, dry weather, covering the mouth and nose with a scarf helps warm and moisten the air before it enters the airways.

Still, it is hard to avoid outdoor triggers, which is why some asthmatics who are allergic to pollen undergo immunotherapy. In immunotherapy small amounts of whatever substance the person is allergic to are injected under the individual's skin. This can include both outdoor and indoor substances that trigger asthma in allergic individuals. At first the allergen is highly diluted so that is does not cause an allergic reaction. Each succeeding injection contains a slightly higher dose. The goal is to gradually desensitize the immune system to the allergen so that it no longer reacts when it is exposed to the substance. This has proven to help reduce allergy symptoms, which, in turn, is thought to lessen the way the airways respond to the substance. According to Plaut, "Allergy shots may reduce your response to the triggers of asthma by causing your body to build up its defenses against certain allergens."[42]

When Emotions or Exercise Trigger Symptoms

Emotionally charged or stressful situations are also difficult to completely avoid. People whose asthma is triggered by emotional factors try to limit their exposure to stressful situations as much as possible. This involves avoiding activities and people who cause them stress.

On the other hand, even though exercise triggers asthma symptoms in some people, most healthcare professionals encourage individuals with asthma to be active, unless they suffer from very severe asthma. Exercise strengthens the body and gives people more energy. This is especially beneficial for individuals with asthma, who often suffer from fatigue caused by asthma attacks. Exercise also strengthens the heart, making it better able to deliver oxygen to the body, and it builds up the chest muscles that can be weakened by persistent asthma attacks. Moreover, exercise reduces stress. Exercise stimulates the body to produce endorphins, natural chemicals that give individuals a feeling of well-being. This helps reduce stress and stress-related asthma symptoms. In addition, there is growing evidence that exercise calms the immune system, allowing

Exercise can trigger asthma symptoms but can also strengthen the body.

the body to suppress the production of chemicals that cause inflammation. St. Louis Rams wide receiver Keenan Burton, who was diagnosed with asthma when he was nine years old, believes that staying active has helped strengthen his body and has made it easier to keep his symptoms under control. "The reason why my asthma is not bad now is because of all the exercising and staying in shape in the past," he explains. "The more active you are, the better chance of overcoming it."[43]

Rather than give up exercise, people with exercise-induced asthma take other steps to lessen the chance of their symptoms arising. The airways of people with exercise-induced asthma start to narrow a few minutes after they begin exercising. To help prevent an asthma attack, healthcare professionals advise susceptible individuals to inhale a dose of their quick-relief bronchodilator before they begin exercising. This keeps the airways from narrowing while the individual exercises. Asthma expert Williams Silvers explains: "My approach is to encourage kids to go for it…. We should be able to, with the medicines that

Physical Effects of Asthma

Asthma can take a toll on the body leading to long-term problems. Frequent asthma attacks make individuals more susceptible to disease. When the body repeatedly gets less oxygen than it needs, every cell in the body is forced to work harder to compensate. Over time, this can weaken the whole body and make people with asthma more susceptible to contracting other diseases. Chronic inflammation, too, can stress the body and make it more vulnerable to disease. In addition, over a period of time, inflammatory chemicals can erode the lining of the lungs, destroying and damaging cells.

Frequent asthma attacks can lead to a barrel-chested appearance. People with asthma repeatedly use muscles to breathe that people without asthma use only after strenuous exercise. These muscles, which surround the neck, ribs, collarbone, and breastbone, help expand the rib cage in order to allow more air to be taken in. When these muscles are used often, the lungs become permanently overinflated and the chest becomes contorted, resulting in a barrel-chested appearance.

we have, pretreat them with a bronchodilator prior to exercise and kids ought to do well."[44]

In addition to taking a quick-relief medicine, individuals with exercise-induced asthma make a point of warming up before they start exercising. Although warming up is important for everyone, for people with exercise-induced asthma, it not only helps get the muscles ready for exercise, it also helps prepare the lungs for the stress. According to Silvers,

It's very important for kids to warm up because we know that with a slow warm-up the lungs get ready regarding the heat and water loss [reduced heat and moisture in the airways trigger exercise-induced asthma]. The lungs acclimate, so you don't have the rapid heat and water loss, and you don't have the sudden onset of exercise-induced asthma. It takes about six minutes. The warm up is very helpful to get the lungs ready for the serious exercise.[45]

There are also certain sports that are less likely to trigger exercise-induced asthma than others. Choosing activities that do not involve exposure to cold, dry air helps. Water sports, in which individuals breathe in warm moist air, are a good option. Because swimming involves controlled breathing, which strengthens the lungs, it is often recommended. In fact, a 2009 study at Tapei Medical University in Singapore divided asthmatic children into two groups. One group underwent a six-week swimming program while the other did not. At the end of the six weeks and for a year thereafter, the subjects in the swimming group experienced a reduction in asthma symptoms, emergency room visits, and school absences. The other group did not. Head researcher Wang Jeng-Shin explains: "Unlike other sports, swimming is unlikely to provoke asthma attacks. In addition to improving asthma, swimming promotes normal physical and psychological development, such as increasing lung volume, developing good breathing techniques, and improving general fitness."[46]

Whether it involves taking up an activity like swimming rather than snow skiing, pretreating exercise-induced asthma, taking allergy shots, giving away a beloved pet, or ridding a house of dust mites and mold, it is clear that managing asthma triggers is not easy. It requires people with asthma to make changes to their environment and their lives. Since doing so reduces asthma symptoms and the chance of an attack occurring, most people say it is worth the effort.

Dealing with Asthma Attacks

Although taking the proper medication and managing asthma triggers are vital to controlling asthma symptoms, there is no way to completely prevent an asthma attack from occurring. However, by monitoring their lung function, having an asthma action plan, and maintaining a healthy lifestyle, individuals can take steps to intercept a potential attack, minimize its severity, and cope with it when it occurs.

Using a Peak Flow Meter

People with asthma often feel like their breathing is normal when it is not. This is because most asthmatics do not have noticeable asthma symptoms until their airways narrow significantly. In much the same manner that diabetics track their blood sugar with a blood glucose meter, asthmatics check their lung functions with a device known as a peak flow meter. It allows patients to measure how forcefully air is blown out of the lungs and to monitor changes in their airways, and it alerts them to a potential asthma attack. Once alerted, individuals can take steps to manage their asthma before an attack gets out of control. According to Plaut,

> Your peak flow score often drops before you or your doctor can notice any sign of asthma. Using a meter, you... can tell if your peak flow has dropped five percent. Using

a stethoscope, your doctor may not notice a change in airflow of less than 25 percent. If you check your peak flow, you can tell early that you are having a problem and how serious it is. If you start treatment right away, you can usually avoid care in the ER.[47]

Peak flow meters are handheld tools that resemble small tubes. They are so simple to use that patients as young as five can learn to use them. When individuals blow into a peak flow meter, an indicator moves to a green, yellow, or red color zone, each of which is designated by numbers 0 through 100. Readings in the green zone fall between 80 and 100 and indicate normal lung functions. Readings between 50 and 79 fall in the yellow or caution zone. They warn individuals that their airways are starting to narrow and that asthma symptoms are developing. At this point, patients take quick-relief medicine to pretreat

Breathing into a peak flow meter (spirometer) during a lung function test measures the amount and speed of air that is exhaled. This allows asthmatics to check for potential asthma attacks.

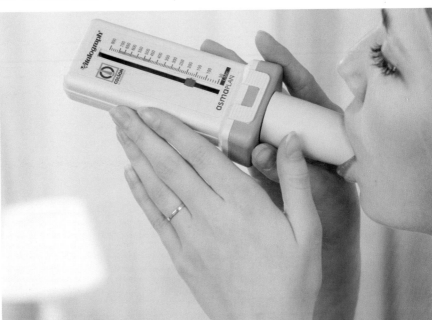

Asthma Through the Ages

Asthma is an ancient disease. An asthmalike disorder was described in ancient Egyptian documents. The Egyptians inhaled fumes emanating from herbs heated on a hot brick to treat the disorder.

The ancient Greeks also described the condition, which they named asthma. It means panting or wheezing in Greek. The Greeks believed asthma was caused by an imbalance in body fluids. They believed that too much of one fluid built up in the airways, thus making it hard to breathe. Centuries later, scientists identified that fluid as mucus. The Greeks prescribed a drink containing owl's blood to loosen the mucus.

Over time, more effective medicines were created to treat asthma but the cause of the disease remained a puzzle. Until the middle of the twentieth century, many people believed that asthma was an emotional rather than a physical illness, which affected nervous, weak, or timid people. In the 1960s, this theory was proven wrong. It is now known that asthma is a physical illness that can affect anyone, including world-class athletes.

This nineteenth-century ad shows a "cure" for asthma.

their symptoms. Consistent yellow readings indicate that individuals do not have adequate control of their asthma and need to consult with their healthcare professional about stepping up a level in their use of long-term controller medication. Readings below 50 fall in the red or danger zone, signaling poor lung function and the start of a severe asthma attack. When this happens, individuals stop what they are doing, immediately take quick-relief medicine, and seek medical attention.

Using a peak flow meter also helps the asthmatic know when it is physically safe to take on big challenges and when it is time to rest. Swimmer Amy Van Dyken, who is both an asthmatic and the winner of six Olympic gold medals, explains:

> Before I got my asthma under control with the right medicines—at age 23—I was rushed to the hospital monthly. Finally I switched medicines and started sleeping through the night. I also got a peak flow meter to measure lung capacity. If I was in the green, I'd go all out and do a normal swim practice. If I was in the yellow, I'd warm up slowly, then see if it was green. If it was still in the yellow, the workout would be less intense. If I got to the pool and was in the red, I wouldn't set foot in the water.[48]

A Peak Flow Chart

Many asthmatics graph their peak flow readings on a special chart designed for this purpose. It provides individuals with a clear visual guide to how well they are managing their condition. Like a peak flow meter, the tri-colored chart features green, yellow, and red zones. Plaut explains: "The graphic design displays peak flow trends at a glance. This prompts you to take action early."[49]

Before patients begin charting their readings, they establish their personal best peak flow rate. To determine it, patients take a peak flow reading twice a day for about a week after effective step-up therapy has their asthma symptoms under control. The highest number is the patient's personal best peak flow rate. Individuals record this number on their peak flow chart. By comparing all future readings to their best peak flow rate, asthmatics can tell how well their asthma is controlled.

Making this comparison also provides individuals with additional warnings about the possibility of an asthma attack. For example, even if an individual's readings are in the green zone, but they show a steady decline or are quite a bit less than the patient's personal best reading, this is a good indicator that something is amiss. Individuals can then take early action to help head off a potential attack.

An Asthma Action Plan

Having and following an asthma action plan (also called an asthma self-management plan) is another tool that helps people with asthma manage their condition and cope during an asthma attack. An asthma action plan is a written plan that patients develop with their doctor. It tells patients what triggers to avoid, names and dosages of all their medications, when and how they should be taken, how to adjust medicines in response to different signs or symptoms, and a list of emergency contact numbers.

Every patient's plan is different. To make following the plan simple, asthma action plans are organized around peak flow reading color zones. Plans tell patients what medication, if any, they should take if they are in the green, yellow, or red zone, what symptoms to watch for in each zone, what actions to take when these symptoms arise, when to seek professional help, and when to go directly to an emergency room. In addition, most plans have a space for patients to record where all their asthma medications are kept and when their prescriptions should be refilled. "The objective of asthma self-management is to make the patient aware of how to manage their asthma under expert guidance," explain Arshad and Babu. "The key aspects are patient education, which is provided in a structured way, and a written self-management action plan. Peak flow is monitored regularly and asthmatic individuals are made aware of their symptoms. This helps to keep their asthma under good control and to act early when deterioration of their conditions begins."[50]

Patients are encouraged to share their asthma action plans with their families, friends, teachers, coaches, and school nurses. That way, should an asthma attack threaten or strike, everyone involved with the patient knows what steps to take. That is why Chad Brown shares his action plan with the Washington Redskins medical staff. He explains: "I have a very clear plan and everyone here on the medical staff knows it, in case I forget and don't have my medications with me, they have them. So yeah, we are always prepared and the plan is very clear to me."[51]

As an individual's asthma changes, so too, do their action plans. Patients typically review their asthma action plans with their doctor at least once a year, and as their medications and dosages change, adjustments are made to the action plan.

Avoiding Germs and Illness

Avoiding illness is another way asthmatics cope with asthma attacks. Doing so helps control their symptoms, lessen the severity of asthma attacks, and make it easier to get through an attack.

Protecting the body against respiratory infections is especially vital. Respiratory infections worsen asthma symptoms and cause a prolonged decrease in lung function in people with asthma. Research has shown that germs that cause colds, coughs, and the flu cause a heightened immune response in asthmatics. This results in high levels of inflammation, leading to severe asthma attacks. In fact, respiratory infections are the most frequent cause of asthma attacks in adults. By taking an annual flu shot and practicing social distancing, which means avoiding contact with infected individuals, asthmatics lessen their chances of developing a respiratory infection. U.S. Congresswoman (NH) Carol Shea Porter's husband and two children have asthma. "I used to just beg people to stay away when they had a cold," she explains. "Because a cold for most people

Avoiding cold and flu germs is vital to asthmatics. Washing hands and wearing respiratory masks while in public can help lessen the instances of respiratory infection.

is a seven-day event, but a cold for my child with asthma would become a two-month odyssey."[52]

Social distancing also involves avoiding crowded public places such as shopping malls, movie theaters, airports, and commuter trains during flu season, as well as avoiding contact with items infected people may have touched. Cold and flu viruses can linger on hard surfaces for days and can be spread through contact with contaminated items. Touching a surface that is infected with the virus, then touching one's mouth or nose spreads the virus. To be safe, during flu season it is best for asthmatics to avoid public restrooms, telephones, water fountains, and pens provided for customers' use in stores, restaurants, and doctor's offices. A shared pen is passed to dozens of people in any given day and is an excellent carrier of respiratory viruses. By simply using their own pens, people with asthma can limit their exposure to respiratory infections and therefore, their risk of a severe asthma attack.

Because it is not always possible for individuals to avoid contact with infected individuals or contaminated items, other common sense health practices can provide protection. Hand washing, for example, is a good way to protect oneself from contracting a respiratory infection. People can accumulate germs that cause respiratory infections on their hands through contact with infected individuals or contaminated surfaces. Proper hand washing with soap and warm water after contact with sick people or while in public places loosens germs on the hands and rinses them away. When soap and water are not

Asthma Camps

Many children with asthma attend special summer camps for kids with asthma. The camps, which are sponsored by the American Lung Association, provide juvenile asthma patients a chance to have fun while developing asthma management skills. With the help of counselors and other campers, they develop plans to avoid asthma triggers, receive instruction and practice using their inhalers correctly, and learn breathing and relaxation techniques to help them handle an asthma attack without panicking.

The campers also share their experiences. This gives them a chance to express their feelings about having asthma and provide each other with information and encouragement. By sharing their common experiences, campers often find solutions to problems that people without asthma do not understand.

In addition, campers participate in physical activities that strengthen their lungs, such as swimming, yoga, and tai chi, as well as other fun activities like archery, softball, and boating, under the supervision of a medical staff.

available, an alcohol-based sanitizer is a good substitute. This is especially important before handling contact lenses and before eating, drinking, or handling food.

In addition, if people with asthma do get a respiratory infection, they are advised to seek help from their healthcare professional rather than trying to treat themselves. Early and aggressive medical treatment can reduce the chances that a respiratory infection will aggravate asthma symptoms.

A Healthy Lifestyle

Maintaining a healthy lifestyle, too, lessens an individual's risk of having an asthma attack, minimizes an attack's severity, and helps people cope during an attack. Getting adequate sleep, for instance, strengthens the body and the immune system, which helps individuals withstand an asthma attack.

In addition, eating a healthy diet strengthens the body and the immune system. Certain foods that seem to reduce inflammation are especially helpful for people with asthma. These include brightly colored fruits and vegetables and foods rich

Foods high in antioxidants, such as apples and grapes, are helpful in protecting the body from damage caused by harmful molecules called free radicals. Many experts believe this damage is a factor in the development of respiratory problems such as asthma.

in omega-3 fatty acids such as salmon, cod, tuna fish, olive oil, nuts, seeds, and wheat germ.

The brightly colored fruits and vegetables contain flavonoids, a group of more than four thousand substances that are believed to have many health benefits, including anti-inflammatory and antioxidant properties. Antioxidants are natural substances that help protect the body against damage caused by oxidation, a process in which cells are weakened when they come in contact with oxygen molecules. Cell damage can aggravate asthma symptoms and make the body less able to fight off respiratory infections.

A 2006 study at Cambridge University examined whether eating fresh fruit offers protection against asthma. It compared the diets of 1,100 adults, half of whom had asthma and half who did not. The study found that those subjects who ate the greatest quantity of fresh fruits were the least likely to have asthma.

The study went on to analyze whether eating fruit had any effect on the frequency and severity of asthma symptoms among the subjects with asthma. It found that those subjects with asthma who ate the most fruit reported fewer asthma attacks than those who ate the least. A number of other studies have come up with comparable findings.

One flavonoid in particular, quercetin, which is found in apples, onions, berries, grapes, and green tea, has caught the eye of scientists around the world. It appears to inhibit the release of inflammatory chemicals that cause the airways to narrow. A number of studies have looked at the effect of quercetin on asthmatic airways. Two Brazilian studies in 2007 and 2010 treated mice with a chemical that caused their airways to become inflamed. Then, one group of mice was administered quercetin, while the other group acted as a control. Airway inflammation was measured in both groups. In both studies, the airways of the mice treated with quercetin were less constricted and less inflamed while there was no significant improvement in the control group.

Conversely, foods high in fat and sodium (salt), such as fast-food hamburgers and french fries, appear to worsen airway inflammation. A 2010 Australian study measured markers of airway inflammation and the lung function of asthmatics before and after the subjects were fed a meal of fast-food burgers and french fries. The subjects' lung function decreased and markers of inflammation increased after eating the high fat meal.

A similar 2010 University of Alberta, Canada, study concluded that eating fast food more than once a week intensifies asthma symptoms. "Fast foods contain high levels of sodium that can increase the risk for wheezing, more twitchy airways and hyper-reactive lungs,"[53] says Canadian researcher Anita Kozyrskyj. Therefore, limiting consumption of these foods may help asthmatics minimize worsening airway inflammation. And, if asthma symptoms are flaring up, avoiding these foods may help reduce the severity of an attack.

Maintaining a Healthy Body Weight

Eating a healthy diet also impacts a person's weight. Maintaining a healthy body weight helps people with asthma lessen the frequency and severity of asthma attacks. Approximately 75 percent of emergency room visits for asthma are among obese individuals. Obesity is a disorder in which individuals have a body mass index greater than or equal to thirty, which makes them severely overweight. Body mass index is a calculation that uses a person's height and weight to estimate how much body fat he or she has.

Research has shown that obese people have poorer lung function than average weight people. The lungs of obese individuals are small in comparison to their body size and therefore have to work harder than those of people who weigh less.

To make matters worse, obese individuals suffer from chronic low-level inflammation throughout their bodies, which negatively impacts asthma symptoms. Their weight also leads to problems in determining accurate dosing of asthma medication and appears to inhibit the effect of some medications.

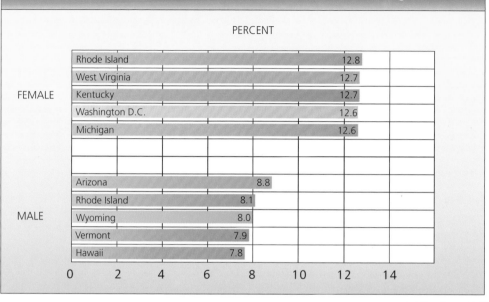

States with Highest Prevalence of Asthma By Gender

PERCENT

		PERCENT
FEMALE	Rhode Island	12.8
	West Virginia	12.7
	Kentucky	12.7
	Washington D.C.	12.6
	Michigan	12.6
MALE	Arizona	8.8
	Rhode Island	8.1
	Wyoming	8.0
	Vermont	7.9
	Hawaii	7.8

0   2   4   6   8   10   12   14

DATA SOURCE: 2008 Adult Asthma Data: Prevalence Tables and Maps, Adult Self-Reported Current Asthma Prevalence Rate (Percent), by Sex and State or Territory. http://www.cdc.gov/asthma/brfss/08/current/tableC21.htm.

A 2008 National Jewish Health, Denver, study determined that corticosteroids are 41 percent less effective in obese and overweight people. According to the researchers, corticosteroids stimulate the production of a chemical known as MKP-1, which interferes with the inflammatory process. When the researchers applied corticosteroids to blood cell cultures taken from obese and non-obese subjects with asthma, they found the medication increased MKP-1 levels in the obese subjects by 3.11 times, compared to 5.27 times in the other subjects. "Steroids were clearly less effective in overweight and obese asthma patients,"[54] explains head researcher Rand Sutherland.

Not surprisingly, obese asthmatics have more severe cases of asthma and more frequent attacks than leaner people. Studies have shown that when obese asthmatics lose weight, they usually gain much better control of their asthma symptoms.

The American Lung Association's Open Airways For Schools program educates children on asthma self-management. It teaches children with asthma ages 8-11 how to detect the warning signs of asthma.

Staying Calm During an Asthma Attack

Despite patients' best efforts to derail asthma attacks before they start, attacks still occur. By staying calm during an attack, individuals can help to minimize the severity of the attack and better cope with what is happening. Having an asthma attack can be very frightening. When individuals panic, stress causes physiological changes in the body, which causes the body to release inflammatory chemicals that worsen the severity of an asthma attack. In addition, when people panic they often hyperventilate. Hyperventilating makes it harder for asthmatics to catch their breath and get air in and out of their narrowed airways. Elyse, a 12-year-old asthmatic, explains: "I have had asthma since I was four. I was just in the hospital because I was hyperventilating….I try to keep my asthma from coming back.

The attacks make me feel like I will never breathe again. I need help to find ways to control the attacks."[55]

Learning to stay calm during an asthma attack gives individuals more control. Doing so is so important that the American Lung Association offers a special program known as Open Airways that teaches children with asthma the relaxation skills and specific breathing exercises that help keep hyperventilation under control. There are many different relaxation exercises. A popular one involves systematically contracting and releasing muscles throughout the body. This exercise helps individuals know how to relax their body during an asthma attack.

Visualization and meditation are two other popular relaxation techniques. Both use the mind to calm the body and reduce feelings of panic. In meditation, individuals use concentration techniques, such as silently repeating a word or chant, to clear the mind in order to relax the body and reduce stress. Research shows that levels of inflammatory chemicals that the body produces as a response to stress decrease during meditation sessions. Scientists are not certain why this is so.

Visualization is similar to meditation. While practicing visualization, individuals envision a special place that makes them feel happy and safe, such as a favorite vacation spot, a tropical beach, or a special event such as a happy family gathering, in order to bring on a relaxed state of mind. Individuals may also envision themselves having an asthma attack without losing control. When an attack actually happens, individuals calm themselves by thinking about their visions.

There is no doubt that having an asthma attack can be very scary. Although there is no way for people with asthma to completely prevent an asthma attack from occurring, remaining calm during an attack, maintaining a healthy lifestyle, using a peak flow meter, and planning for emergencies will help individuals gain control over their condition and their lives.

CHAPTER FIVE

The Future of Asthma

Scientists are investigating possible causes of asthma. They hope to use the knowledge they gain to help prevent the development of new cases of asthma in the future. In order to help people with asthma right away, scientists are working on developing new and improved treatments.

Exposure to Dangerous Chemicals Before Birth

Scientists know that when a fetus is exposed to a harmful substance, it can affect the fetus's development and the baby's health after birth. Any substance that enters a pregnant woman's bloodstream is transmitted to the developing fetus through the placenta, a tube-like structure through which the fetus receives oxygen and nutrition. Consequently, the fetus is exposed to everything that enters the mother's blood, whether by mouth, air, or intravenously.

Alcohol, medications, illegal drugs, contaminated food, and various chemicals all can adversely affect an unborn baby. This is because fetal cells are undeveloped and fragile, making the fetus especially sensitive and vulnerable to the effects of different substances.

Scientists are looking at whether fetal exposure to one particular chemical, Bisphenol A, commonly abbreviated as BPA, can lead to the development of asthma. BPA is found in some plastic containers and in the lining of some aluminum cans. Different animal tests have shown that exposure to BPA can affect brain and sexual development in fetal mice and rats. Given this, scientists theorized that the chemical might also negatively

The lining of some aluminum cans contain measurable levels of
Bisphenol A (BPA). BPA has been linked to various forms of ill health,
including asthma.

impact the development of fetal airways and may be linked to
the development of asthma.

To test this theory, in 2010 researchers at the University of
Texas Medical Branch at Galveston, put 0, 1, or 10 micrograms
per milliliter doses of BPA in the drinking water of three groups
of female mice before, during, and after pregnancy while the
mice were nursing. According to the scientists, the largest dose
of 10 micrograms per milliliter of BPA was comparable to what
a human fetus might be exposed to.

Four days after the mice gave birth, the babies were injected
with an allergen to make them more susceptible to asthma.
Then, the researchers measured the level of inflammatory
chemicals in all the babies' lungs and their lung functions. The
mice born to the mothers who were exposed to 10 micrograms
of BPA developed significant signs of asthma including high levels of inflammation and poor lung function. The other groups
did not develop asthma symptoms.

Since human airways may not react in exactly the same manner, the results of the study are not conclusive evidence that

fetal exposure to BPA can cause asthma, but they do point in that direction. Erik Forno of the University of Miami Miller School of Medicine explains: "The mice they used are very well-accepted models for asthma and allergies so it should be a very good model of what we would expect to happen in humans."[56]

To determine the effect of the chemical on humans, the scientists have begun tests using human umbilical cord blood samples. At the same time, a number of U.S. health care agencies have pledged more than 30 million dollars to fund further research on the health effects of BPA.

Based on what is already known, the FDA recommends that parents take steps to limit infant exposure to BPA, and some doctors are advising expectant mothers to avoid using products containing the chemical. Currently, twenty states and four cities have proposed bans on products containing BPA. In 2010, Connecticut was the first state to pass a law banning the use of the chemical in all reusable food and beverage containers and in infant formula and baby food containers. Many stores have removed from their shelves such products as plastic baby bottles and pacifiers made with BPA.

If further studies prove that fetal exposure to BPA does, indeed, lead to the development of asthma, it is likely the chemical will be banned, which should help lessen the prevalence of asthma cases in the future.

Acetaminophen

Another chemical, acetaminophen, a common ingredient in over-the-counter pain, fever, and cold remedies, has caught the interest of other researchers. In 2009, scientists at Columbia University in New York studied what effect fetal exposure to acetaminophen has on the development of asthma in children. The researchers compared acetaminophen use during pregnancy in 301 women to the prevalence of asthma symptoms in their children at five years old.

The mothers were surveyed about how frequently they used acetaminophen during their pregnancy, how frequently their children wheezed, and how frequently the children had visited

Acetaminophen may relieve back pain or muscle ache during pregnancy. However, researchers have found that mothers who use acetaminophen during their pregnancy can increase their child's risk of asthma-related illnesses.

an emergency room for respiratory problems. The researchers found that 34 percent of the mothers used acetaminophen during their pregnancy, and 27 percent of the children had asthma. The children whose mothers used acetaminophen were more likely to wheeze and were more likely to visit the emergency room for respiratory problems than the children of nonusers. Moreover, the risk increased as the number of days of prenatal exposure to the chemical increased. A similar study in Great Britain came up with similar results. "These findings…suggest caution in the use of acetaminophen during pregnancy,"[57] says lead researcher Matthew S. Perzanowski.

Scientists at the Medical Research Institute in Wellington, New Zealand, have also been looking at the link between acetaminophen and asthma. Rather than investigating whether fetal exposure to the chemical raises asthma risk, they examined whether teenagers who take acetaminophen are more likely to develop asthma than their peers who do not take acetaminophen. In 2010, the researchers looked at 320,000 subjects in fifty countries. The subjects were surveyed about how often they took acetaminophen and their history of asthma. The researchers found that the subjects who took acetaminophen at least once a month were 2.5 times more likely to have asthma symptoms than the subjects who never took the drug. Subjects who took acetaminophen just once a year were still 40 percent more likely to have asthma than those who did not use the drug. In 2008, the same research team conducted a similar study on younger children. That study found that children who were treated with acetaminophen as infants were more likely to develop asthma by age six than children who did not receive the drug.

Since neither study used a control group, the scientists cannot say for sure whether taking acetaminophen actually causes asthma. It is also unclear how acetaminophen affects asthma symptoms. Some experts think the drug triggers the production of a chemical that encourages an inflammatory response in the airways. To help learn more, further studies are planned.

If additional studies confirm a connection between acetaminophen use and the development of asthma, it is likely that pregnant women, infants, children, and teenagers may be warned against using it. This would help reduce future asthma cases. Until then, some healthcare professionals are advising their patients to cut back on their acetaminophen use. According to asthma expert Harold Nelson of National Jewish Health, Denver, "It would be prudent [wise] for parents to avoid the use of acetaminophen in their kids. The evidence has been building for a while and it is very, very, convincing."[58]

Stress During Pregnancy

Other scientists are investigating whether a stressful pregnancy increases a baby's chances of developing asthma. Previous animal studies have shown that prenatal stress can negatively affect the development of the fetal immune system. In 2010, Harvard University scientists undertook a human study. They questioned a total of 557 pregnant women about the amount and type of stress in their lives, including questions about financial worries, family problems, and crime in their communities. In each of the families surveyed, one of the parents had asthma and/or allergies. As a result, each of the babies had a similar, but not exact, genetic risk of developing asthma.

When the babies were born, the scientists took umbilical cord blood samples, which they tested with different allergens. The babies born to the mothers who reported being under the most stress produced the highest level of an inflammatory chemical associated with airway constriction and asthma. In comparison, babies born to the least stressed mothers produced very low levels of the chemical. Lead researcher Rosalind Wright explains:

This is the first human study to corroborate [support] research from animal studies demonstrating stress experienced by mothers during pregnancy influences the child's developing immune system starting in the womb....The cytokine [inflammatory chemical] patterns seen in the higher-stress groups, an indicator of how the child's immune system is functioning at birth and responding to the environment, may be a marker of increased risk for developing asthma as they get older.[59]

To see if the subjects do, indeed, develop asthma, the researchers plan to track the children's respiratory symptoms as they grow. If follow-up studies prove that prenatal stress can cause asthma, it is likely that stress reduction will become an important element in the care of expectant mothers. "The work," Wright says, "may point to the need to design interventions and strategies to reduce stress in pregnant women to both enhance the mother's well-being and to reduce the risk of chronic illnesses in their children, such as asthma."[60]

Can Air Pollution Cause Asthma?

Still other scientists are taking another tactic. They are looking at environmental factors that may cause asthma. One such factor is air pollution. Scientists already know that air pollution can irritate the airways of both asthmatics and nonasthmatics, and that asthma is widespread in inner cities where air pollution is greatest. Based on these factors, a number of scientists have been investigating whether exposure to high levels of air pollution may actually cause asthma to develop in children. Children are the focus of these studies because their lungs are

not fully developed and are therefore more vulnerable to harmful chemicals than those of adults.

The Children's Health Study, a long-term study in which the first phase took place from 1992 to 2004, and has since been continued, is the longest and one of the most important studies into the link between air pollution and the development of asthma. The first phase of the study, which is sponsored by the California Air Resources Board, monitored the lung function and the frequency of respiratory problems of 5,500 school-age children in eighty-six different South California communities. Depending on where they lived, the children were exposed to varying levels of air pollution. The scientists measured concentrations of different pollutants that the children were exposed to and compared this data to the children's lung function rates and the frequency of any respiratory problems they had.

A view of the smog over Los Angeles, California. Studies in Southern California showed that children in communities with higher levels of pollution had higher occurences of asthma.

When school buses leave their engines running while waiting for students, they can increase air pollution around the school and in the bus.

The scientists found that the children living in the communities with the highest levels of pollution were three to five times more likely to have below normal lung function rates than the children living in communities with lower levels of pollution. They also found that new cases of asthma were most likely to occur among the children who were exposed to high levels of ozone, a substance that is created when exhaust fumes from cars and trucks are exposed to sunlight. Rates were highest among those children who played sports outdoors in high-ozone areas. In fact, young athletes in the high-ozone communities were three times more likely to develop asthma than their peers in low-ozone communities. The scientists think that the airways of young athletes are especially vulnerable to ozone because athletes generally breathe deeply and rapidly while they are exercising, causing them to inhale about twenty times more pollutants than nonathletes.

The results of the California study were so significant that a second phase was launched to learn more. As part of this study, the scientists found that children who live within a quarter mile of a freeway are 89 percent more likely to develop asthma than children living a mile away.

Across the world, in a similar study, Swedish researchers also looked for a link between traffic pollution and the development of asthma. In 2008, they monitored four thousand children from birth to one year old living in Stockholm and the surrounding countryside to see if exposure to high levels of traffic pollution increased the subjects' chances of developing asthma symptoms. The scientists found that the subjects who were exposed to the highest levels of traffic fumes were 60 percent more likely to have persistent asthma symptoms than the subjects who were not exposed to the pollution.

Secondhand Smoke and Asthma

Smoking is not healthy for anyone. It is especially dangerous for people with asthma. Smoking damages the lungs and causes the airways to become inflamed. Inhaling secondhand smoke is also harmful, especially for children. Because their lungs are not fully developed, children are very vulnerable to the negative effects of this smoke, which contains more than four thousand chemicals. Regularly inhaling secondhand smoke slows the growth of children's lungs and makes them breathe more rapidly than normal, which causes them to inhale even more smoke. It can trigger asthma attacks in susceptible individuals and make asthma symptoms more severe. According to the American Cancer Society, secondhand smoke increases the severity of asthma attacks in 200,000 to one million American children each year.

In addition, secondhand smoke not only causes problems for children with asthma, new findings show it can actually cause healthy children as young as preschool age to develop asthma. The American Lung Association estimates that 8,000 to 26,000 new cases of asthma each year are caused by exposure to secondhand smoke.

As a result of these studies, many different groups are taking steps to reduce the amount of air pollution children are exposed to. These steps range from passing laws that limit the amount of different pollutants factories and motor vehicles emit, requiring motor vehicles to use cleaner fuel, sponsoring research into the development of clean fuel, and building schools and parks far from high traffic areas. Some schools are prohibiting cars and school buses from leaving their engines running as they pick up and drop off students on school grounds. When cars and school buses leave their engines running while they wait for students, it increases air pollution around the school. Dangerous particles also get inside the buses and into classrooms through vents and open windows. Pamela Turner of the University of Georgia, Alpharetta, works with schools to implement the ban. She explains:

A line of idling school buses doesn't just pollute the air around the buses. They also pollute the air in the bus and can emit particulates that can enter the school, reducing the air quality inside too…It takes individuals, families, and communities to change these practices. Each person taking baby steps will add up. If every parent waiting in line to pick up their children turns their car off, it helps.[61]

Such efforts should help reduce future asthma cases. In the meantime, some experts advise families with young children to avoid living close to freeways and major roads. And young athletes are advised to forego exercising outdoors on ozone alert days.

New Treatments

While some scientists are investigating possible causes of asthma in order to prevent new cases from developing, others are working on developing new and better treatments to help people now. One new treatment is aimed at helping people with severe persistent asthma. While current asthma medications

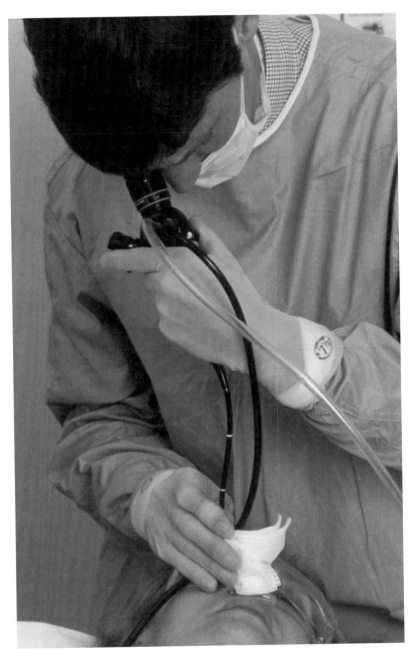

In a bronchial thermoplasty, a bronchoscope, which has a tiny camera attached, is passed through a patient's mouth or nose. The camera allows the doctor to see into the patient's airways.

help most people, it is harder to get this level under control. As a result, people with severe persistent asthma take stronger and more frequent doses of asthma medication than people with less severe asthma. This increases their risk of experiencing harmful side effects. One new treatment, known as bronchial thermoplasty, helps people with severe persistent asthma to get their symptoms under control.

Bronchial thermoplasty involves using radio waves to heat the muscle walls that surround the airways in the lungs. The heat permanently reduces the thickness of the muscle walls, thus making them less constricted, which helps the patient to breathe more easily. During this procedure, a tiny tube attached to a device known as a bronchoscope is passed through the patient's mouth or nose into the airways. A camera on the bronchoscope allows the doctor to see inside via a computer screen. The tip of the tube delivers radio waves to the muscles surrounding the airways. The radio waves are about the same temperature as a warm cup of coffee, which is hot enough to cause the muscles to relax without burning or scarring them.

The procedure is performed over three hour-long sessions. Each time, the patient's airways are numbed to minimize any discomfort. A clinical trial, which is a test using human subjects, on 297 patients with severe asthma proved so successful that in 2010 the FDA approved the use of bronchial thermoplasty for the treatment of patients eighteen years old or older with severe persistent asthma. Patients in the trial showed a 32 percent reduction in asthma attacks and an 84 percent decrease in emergency room visits. In order to study the treatment's long-term safety and effectiveness, the health of the patients who were involved in the clinical trial as well as that of any new patients who receive the treatment will be tracked and studied for five years. If all goes well, the treatment will become readily available by 2015.

Help from Vitamin D

Other scientists are investigating another treatment option. They are studying what role vitamin D, which is important in

Black Currants May Help Control Asthma

A 2010 study by scientists in New Zealand has shown that a substance found in black currants may help control asthma symptoms. Black currants are grapelike fruits that are high in vitamins and antioxidants. They also contain a substance known as epigallocatechin, which appears to have anti-inflammatory properties. The scientists wondered what effect, if any, epigallocatechin has on asthmatic airways.

To find out, the scientists treated lung tissue with an allergen, which caused the tissue to become inflamed. Then they applied an extract made of epigallocatechin to the tissue and recorded the reaction. The extract significantly reduced the inflammation. The scientists think that chemicals in the extract work with the body's own chemicals to turn off uncontrolled inflammation.

More research is needed to learn exactly how epigallocatechin affects the body. In an effort to limit the body's reaction to allergens and asthma triggers, in the future scientists may enrich foods with epigallocatechin and use it in new asthma medications.

Black currants have anti-inflammatory properties that may help control asthma symptoms.

the development of the lungs and immune system, may play in lessening asthma symptoms. A 2009 Harvard Medical School study looked at 616 Costa Rican school children with asthma to see if there was a link between blood calcium levels and asthma symptoms. To find out, the scientists measured the children's lung functions and vitamin D blood levels, and compared this data to how often the children's parents reported that the children had asthma symptoms. The scientists found that the children with the lowest levels of vitamin D had the poorest lung function and the most frequent asthma symptoms.

Another 2009 study, sponsored by Children's Medical Center in Washington, D.C., reported similar findings. In this study, the vitamin D blood levels of 85 African American children with asthma and 21 healthy African American children were measured. The study found that the children with asthma were twenty times more likely to have low levels of vitamin D than the healthy children.

Further studies are needed to see what effect raising vitamin D levels may have on asthma symptoms. A 2009 Jikei University School of Medicine (Tokyo, Japan) study that looked at whether taking a daily vitamin D supplement would lessen a group of children's chances of contracting a cold or the flu came up with some interesting results. Although asthma was not the focus of the study, the researchers noted that during the course of the study, the subjects with asthma who received vitamin D supplements had significantly fewer asthma attacks than the asthmatic subjects in the control group. As a result, the researchers are planning another study focusing on asthma.

If the results of the new study show the same effect, it is likely that vitamin D supplements will become a part of asthma treatment. Other new treatments are also on the horizon. In fact, it is possible that someday scientists will develop a vaccine to prevent asthma. Right now, what is being learned should give people with asthma more control over the disease and reduce asthma cases in the future.

Notes

Introduction: A Common Problem

1. Quoted in Leah Fabel, "Credo: Chris Draft," *The Examiner*, July 18, 2010. www.washingtonexaminer.com/local/98617624.htm.
2. Quoted in "61st World Health Assembly," World Health Organization, May 19-24, 2008. www.who.int/respiratory/asthma/WHA_2008/en/index.html.
3. Quoted in "Kyle Clark and Family Tackle Asthma in Toronto," Chris Draft Family Foundation, November 30, 2009. www.chrisdraftfamilyfoundation.org/news_media/articles?id=0093.
4. Sarah Newman, "Air Pollution: Not Just Someone Else's Problem," Fav Stocks, July 31, 2010. www.favstocks.com/air-pollution-not-just-someone-else%E2%80%99s-problem/3021890/.
5. Quoted in Asthma Personal Stories, Penn Medicine. www.pennmedicine.org/health_info/asthma/000132.html.
6. Quoted in "The Gable Family," Chris Draft Family Foundation. www.chrisdraftfamilyfoundation.org/initiatives/asthmateam/tell/?id=0014.

Chapter One: Overly Sensitive Airways

7. Quoted in "New Program May Help Manage Asthma Symptoms," WJZ.com, October 21, 2008. http://wjz.com/sports/asthma.2.845666.html.
8. S. Hasan Arshad and K. Suresh Babu, *The Facts: Asthma*. Oxford, England: Oxford University Press, 2009, p. 38.
9. William E. Berger, MD, MBA, *Asthma for Dummies*. Hoboken, NJ: Wiley Publishing, 2006, p. 12.
10. Mehmet Oz, "What Does an Asthma Attack Feel Like," Ask Dr. Oz. http://ask.doctoroz.com/question/what-does-asthma-feel-like.
11. Wheezy, "Readers Respond How is Asthma for You? -

Sports and No One Knows." About.com: Asthma, www.
asthma.about.com/u/ua/asthmabasics/ua_scary.htm.
12. Julia, interview with the author, New York City, June 13,
2010.
13. Gabby Farmer, "Life with Asthma and Allergies: Straight
Talk for AANMA's Teen Ambassadors: A Good Day Goes
Bad—In a Cloud of Smoke," AANMA.org, June 30, 2010.
www.aanma.org/2010/06/life-with-asthma-and-allergies-
straight-talk-from-aanma%e2%80%99s-teen-ambassadors/.
14. Arshad and Babu, *The Facts: Asthma*, p. 104.
15. Quoted in Tara Parker-Pope, "Asthma Attacks Linked
With Weather," New York Times, September 22, 2009.
www.well.blogs.nytimes.com/2009/09/22/asthma-
problems-linked-with-weather-changes.
16. "Sports and Asthma: Mom I Can't Breathe," Everyday
Health. www.everydayhealth.com/asthma/webcasts/
sports-and-asthma-mom-i-cant-breathe-transcript-1.aspx.
17. Sara Reistad-Long, "The Hidden Cause of Disease," *Pa-
rade's Healthy Style*, July/August 2010, p. 6.
18. "The Kazsa Family," Chris Draft Family Foundation,
www.chrisdraftfamilyfoundation.org/initiatives/
asthmateam/tell?id=001.
19. "The Kazsa Family," Chris Draft Family Foundation.
20. Marcel Lemire, "Asthma: Personal Stories The Faces of
Asthma," The Lung Association. www.lung.ca/diseases-
maladies/asthma-asthme/faces-visages/marcel_e.php.

Chapter Two: Diagnosis and Treatment
21. Arshad and Babu, *The Facts: Asthma*, p. 51.
22. Quoted in Asthma Personal Stories Nancy Hogshead,"
Penn Medicine. www. pennmedicine.org/health_info/
asthma/0000132.html.
23. Berger, *Asthma for Dummies*, p. 35.
24. Berger, *Asthma for Dummies*, p. 36.
25. Arshad and Babu, *The Facts: Asthma*, p. 80.
26. Arshad and Babu, *The Facts: Asthma*, p. 79.
27. John-Henry Lambin, "Life with Asthma and Allergies:
Straight Talk from AANMA's Teen Ambassadors – A
Sage(brush) Solution," AANMA.org, June 30, 2010. www.
aanma.org/2010/06/life-with-asthma-and-allergies-straight-

talk-from-aanma%e2%80%99s-teen-ambassadors/.

28. Quoted in "South Dakota is 50th State to Protect Rights to Carry and Self-Administer Asthma Medication," Allergy and Asthma Network Mothers of Asthmatics, March 2, 2010. www.aanma.org/2010/03/south-dakota-is-50th-state-to-protect-students%e2%80%99-rights-to-carry-and-self-administer-asthma-medication/.

29. Thomas F. Plaut, M.D., *One Minute Asthma*. Amherst, MA: Pedipress, Inc, 2008. p. 73.

30. Julia, interview with the author.

31. Quoted in "FDA Considers Safety of 12-Hour Bronchodilators." Allergy and Asthma Network Mothers of Asthmatics, March 27, 2009. www.aanma.org/2009/03/fda-considers-safety-of-12-hour-bronchodilators/.

32. Quoted in "FDA Considers Safety of 12-Hour Bronchodilators," Allergy and Asthma Network Mothers of Asthmatics.

Chapter Three: Managing Asthma Triggers

33. Berger, *Asthma for Dummies*, p. 90.

34. Quoted in Celebrities with Asthma: Chad Brown," Cure Autoimmunity, September 2, 2009. www.cureautoimmunity.org/celebrities-with-asthma-chad-brown.

35. Berger, *Asthma for Dummies*, p. 92.

36. Quoted in Amy, "Asthma Mom's 10 Rules to De-Trigger Your Home," Asthma Mom, June 16, 2010. www.theasthmamom.com/2010/06/16/asthma-moms-10-rules-to-de-trigger-your-house/.

37. Quoted in Melanie D.G. Kaplan, "FiveYears Post-Katrina: Record Asthma Numbers Led To New Program," Smart Planet, August 25, 2010. www.smartplanet.com/people/blog/pure-genius/five-years-post-katrina-record-asthma-numbers-led-to-new-program/4426.

38. Quoted in Laura Kirtley, "Asthma Rates On the Rise," WLFI.com, May 4, 2010. www.wlfi.com/dpp/news/local/Asthma-rates-on-the-rise.

39. Quoted in Lisa Belkin, "When Baby is Allergic to Kitty," New York Times, March 19, 2010. www.parenting.blogs.nytimes.com/2010/03/19/when-baby-is-allergic-to-kitty/.

40. Julia, interview with the author.

41. "Living with Asthma? A Short Essay," Matt'swire Blog, July 2010. www.richmondjoke.typepad.com/blog/2010/07/ living-with-asthma-a-short-essay.html.

42. Plaut, *One Minute Asthma*, p. 19.

43. Quoted in "St. Louis Ram Keenan Burton Tackling Asthma," Chris Draft Family Foundation, January 3, 2010. www.chrisdraftfamilyfoundation.org/news_media/ articles?id=0117.

44. Quoted in "Sports and Asthma: Mom, I Can't Breathe," Everyday Health.

45. Quoted in "Sports and Asthma: Mom, I Can't Breathe," Everyday Health.

46. Quoted in "Swimming Aids Asthma Symptoms in Children, Study Finds," Science Daily, August 27, 2009. www. sciencedaily.com/releases/2009/08/090824205522.htm.

Chapter Four: Dealing with Asthma Attacks

47. Plaut, *One Minute Asthma*, p. 28.

48. Quoted in Anne Stein, "Exclusive Interview: Breathless in Sydney," A Healthy Me. www.ahealthyme.com/topic/ asthmaqa.

49. Plaut, *One Minute Asthma*, p. 32.

50. Arshad and Babu, *The Facts: Asthma*, p. 103.

51. Quoted in "Celebrities with Asthma: Chad Brown," Cure Autoimmunity.

52. Quoted in "From House to the Home," AANMA.org, June 1, 2010. www.aanma.org/2010/06/from-home-to-the-house/.

53. Quoted in Sharon Kirkey, "Higher Asthma Rates Linked to Fast Food," The Windsor Star. www.windsorstar.com/ health/Higher+asthma+rates+linked+fast+food/1226588/ story.html.

54. Quoted in "Steroids Not as Effective in Obese Asthma Patients," Science Daily, September 18, 2008. www. sciencedaily.com/releases/2008/09/080916215217.htm.

55. Quoted in "Asthma," The American Lung Association in Washington. www.alaw.org/asthma.

Chapter Five: The Future of Asthma

56. Quoted in Amanda Gardner, "BPA May Raise Risk of Asthma for Kids," MSN Health and Fitness, February 28, 2010. www.health.msn.com/health-topics/asthma/articlepage.aspx?cp-documentid=100254888.

57. Quoted in "Use of Acetaminophen During Pregnancy Associated with Increased Asthma Symptoms in Children," E! Science News, February 4, 2010. www.esciencenews.com/articles/2010/02/04/use.acetaminophen.pregnancy.associated.with.increased.asthma.symptoms.children.

58. Quoted in "Acetaminophen May Double Asthma Risk in Kids," Huffington Post, August 13, 2010. www.huffingtonpost.com/2010/08/13/acetaminophen-may-double_n_681793.html.

59. Quoted in Steven Reinberg, "Prenatal Stress May Boost Baby's Asthma Risk," Business Week, March 18 2010. www.businessweek.com/lifestyle/content/healthday/637111.html.

60. Quoted in Steven Reinberg, "Prenatal Stress May Boost Baby's Asthma Risk."

61. Quoted in J. Faith Peppers, "Idling Buses Bad for Air, Kids," Savannah Now, July 28, 2010. www.savannahnow.com/effingham-now/2010-07-28/idling-buses-bad-air-kids.

Glossary

airways: A road-like network in the lungs through which air travels in and out.

allergen: A harmless substance, such as dust, that the body reacts to inappropriately.

allergy: An overreaction by the immune system to allergens.

anti-inflammatory: A drug used to block inflammation.

antioxidant: A substance that helps the body fight disease.

asthma action plan: A written plan that helps patients to manage asthma symptoms.

asthmatic: A person with asthma.

aveoli: Air sacks in the lungs where oxygen and carbon dioxide are transferred in and out of the blood stream.

bronchial thermoplasty: An asthma treatment that uses radio waves to thin the muscle walls in airways.

bronchi: Two tubes that connect the windpipe to the lungs.

bronchioles: Tiny tubes within the lungs.

bronchodilator: A commonly used medicine that opens the airways during an asthma attack.

corticosteroids: Drugs used to control inflammation.

high efficiency particle arrestor (HEPA): An air filter used in vacuum cleaners and air purifiers that filters out dust mites and other allergens from the air.

hyperresponsive airways: The airways of people with asthma that overreact to substances that do not affect other people.

immune system: The body's disease fighting system.

immunotherapy: Allergy treatment in which small amounts of allergens are injected under an individual's skin to help desensitize the person to the allergens.

inflammation: The body's defense against germs, characterized by heat, swelling, redness, and pain.

inhaler: A device that allows medicine to be delivered directly into the airways.

long-term controller: A drug that is taken long-term to control airway inflammation.

mucus: A thick gooey substance produced by the respiratory system to trap irritants.

nebulizer: A machine that discharges an easy-to-inhale mist of asthma medication into a patient's airways through a face mask or mouthpiece.

peak flow meter: A device that asthmatics use to monitor their lung function.

quick-relief or rescue medicine: Medication used to open the airways during an asthma attack.

spirometer: A device used by doctors to measure lung function.

trigger: A substance or event that provokes an asthma attack.

wheeze: A whistling sound made when individuals try to force air through constricted airways.

windpipe: A long hollow tube through which air travels from the nose or mouth to the lungs.

Organizations to Contact

American Academy of Allergy, Asthma and Immunology
611 Wells St.
Milwaukee, WI 53202-3889
(800) 822-2762
www.aaai.org

This professional organization offers information about asthma and allergies, including lists of doctors, recent news, and an information hotline.

American College of Allergies, Asthma, and Immunology
85 W. Algonquin Rd,. Suite 550
Arlington Heights, IL 60005
(847) 427-1200
www.acaai.org

This professional organization offers information on every aspect of asthma as part of its patient education resources. It also lists doctors and provides recent news.

The American Lung Association
61 Broadway, 6th floor
New York, NY 10006
(800) 548-8252
email: info@lungusa.org
www.lungusa.org

The American Lung Association provides lots of information on asthma. It also supports new research and sponsors local support groups.

Asthma and Allergy Foundation of America
8201 Corporate Drive, Suite 1000
Landover, MD 20785
(800) 727-8462
email: info@aafa.org
www.aafa.org

This organization provides educational material, newsletters, and an asthma information hotline that operates twenty-four hours a day.

For More Information

Books

Carol Ballard, *Lungs*. Chicago: Heinemann, 2010. Information about the respiratory system and the different illnesses that affect it, including asthma.

William E. Berger, *Teen's Guide to Living with Asthma*. NY: Facts on File, 2007. Provides information to help young people cope with asthma.

Hal Marcovitz, *Asthma: Diseases and Disorders*. San Diego: Reference Point Press, 2010. Looks at asthma causes, diagnosis, and treatment, as well as coping with asthma. Includes full-color pictures and statistics.

Alvin Silverstein, Virginia Silverstein, and Laura Silverstein Nunn, *The Asthma Update*. Berkeley Heights, NJ: Enslow, 2006. Looks at asthma symptoms, treatment, history, and current research.

Periodicals

Sanjay Gupta, "Asthma Proof Your Home." *Time Magazine*. June 7, 2006.

Alice Park, "Parental Stress Increases Kids' Asthma Risk." *Time Magazine*. July 22, 2009.

January W. Payne, "Air Pollution and Asthma: 4 Ways to Stay Safe on 'Ozone-Alert' Days." *U.S. News and World Report*. June 11, 2010.

Internet Sources

Mayo Clinic, "Asthma," www.mayoclinic.com/health/asthma/DS00021.

Teens Health, "Asthma," http://teenshealth.org/teen/diseases_conditions/allergies_immune/asthma.html.

Websites

Breathe Easy, Play Hard (www.beph.com/site). This non-profit organization is dedicated to supporting young athletes with asthma. It provides facts about asthma, coping skills for athletes with asthma, and information and interviews with professional athletes with asthma.

Asthma (www.cdc.gov/asthma). This website sponsored by the Centers for Disease Control offers extensive health information about asthma diagnosis and treatment. It also has resources for teachers and schools to provide a better environment for children with asthma.

National Jewish Medical Research Center (www.njc.org). This Denver hospital specializes in treating asthma and allergies. Its website provides lots of information on asthma.

Teen Asthma.ca (www.teenasthma.ca/index.jsp). The Canadian Lung Association sponsors this website. It is geared just for young people and offers lots of information about every aspect of asthma.

Index

Picture Credits

About the Author

Barbara Sheen is the author of more than sixty books for young people. She lives in New Mexico with her family. In her spare time, she likes to swim, walk, cook, and garden.